Lessons in Printing

Lessons in Printing

Printing

A Memoir

by

Klancy Clark de Nevers

Scattered Leaves Press
Salt Lake City, Utah

Poem "Curator" by Klancy Clark de Nevers, originally published in Salt Lake City's *City Weekly* second annual literary issue, Sep. 21, 2000 (Vol. 17, No. 17), as the first place poetry winner. Contest judged by Craig Arnold.

Some of the illustrations and quotes used throughout the book are from *Lessons in Printing, Units of Regular Courses* (International Typographical Union, Indianapolis, Ind., 1928)

Book design and formatting by James W. Warren and Klancy Clark de Nevers.

Cover design by Dan Mabutt

Published by Scattered Leaves Press
358 South 700 East, Suite B, #603
Salt Lake City, UT 84102
www.ScatteredLeavesPress.com

ISBN 978-0-9972076-2-0

For my sisters, Kristine and Kathy,
and our cousin, John Clark

Nothing has a stronger influence...on their children than the unlived life of the parent.

—Carl G. Jung

People make history by passing on gossip, saving old records, and by naming rivers, mountains, and children. Some people leave only their bones, though bones too make a history when someone notices.

—Laurel Thatcher Ulrich

Table of Contents

PROLOGUE

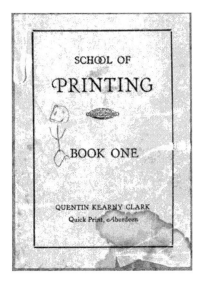

SCHOOL OF

PRINTING

BOOK ONE

QUENTIN KEARNY CLARK
Quick Print, Aberdeen

CURATOR

The moon has moved
to its winter window. The spirits
in the house are restless; old
magazines slump off stacks.

She pokes about in corners, moving boxes,
rustles papers, and thinks of a great-aunt
scribbling notes – where she hid the silver,
who gets the chiming clock,
divesting.

Uncles wait in boxes for their handwriting
to be admired. On a beach the child
who becomes her father, sits
in a dress and straw hat.
Beside his report cards.
.....Also perfect. Voices sift
from the attic. She cannot move
without bruising books inscribed
to someone else. This room
belongs to her father's family, that one
to her husband's, the closet
to an ancestral diary and a daughter's
discarded dress.

She opens the airless Chinese chest
and gasps for breath, recalling
the scent of a mildewed past.
Pulling tight the shabby bathrobe,
she piles hunting trophies on clippings
of tragedies, rearranges cousins,
shuts the door.

Tonight the moon gains apogee.
The cat patrols the hallway,
challenges the shadows
in her house.

The Curator

If a piece of paper gets into my house for a day, I'll save it forever.

Some in my family had a penchant for alcohol. I'm addicted to preservation. So was my mother. My inheritance from her is box after box of memorabilia. When I lugged them into the package store near her last home, the clerk who helped ship them to Utah teased that my mother must have been a rock collector. But really, it was just paper. We've never thrown away postcards, dance cards, opera programs, airplane boarding stubs, birthday cards, train schedules, birth announcements, report cards, children's art, newspaper clippings, books by our relatives, books we plan to read someday. Aunt Barbara saved her long-mourned cat's whiskers, carefully labeled in a jewelry box. We raise the value of mundane things just by nesting them in shoe boxes, stuffing them into picture frames, stacking them in corners or under the stairs. Holding on to them. Letting the ink, and the paper, age, like fine wine.

This preservation project may hold the key to understanding my printer father, and to clarify why, from the time I turned twenty, I wrote my father off as a lost cause.

Librarians call the jumble of personal effects that one gives to an archive *ephemera*. That word makes me laugh. From WordPerfect's dictionary: ephemera–noun–*items of short-lived interest or usefulness, especially those that later acquire value to collectors.* Its Greek origin signifies "things lasting only a day."

In my hand is the physical evidence that in 1941, my father, Kearny Clark, bought a Chrysler Windsor convertible with white sidewall tires for $953 with a trade-in. I remember the freedom of driving that shiny black car—the keys were always in it—the red leather upholstery, the leaky canvas top. My mother saved this receipt for fifty-two years, and I've stored it for another twenty or so. It bears my father's signature, and he probably printed the sale form used by Hahn Motors. How can I throw all that away?

A piece of the EKG printout from Mother's death bed shows the steady but irregular heartbeat that held until her other organs failed. The tape rests in an album beside her leather-bound high school diploma and a poem in spidery writing celebrating her marriage: "...To you he's The Only One.../ So you gained by marrying / without tarrying /...Yours Cordially, Grandmother Cochran."

I regret items that got away from us: Mother's wooden peach box of family photos left behind during a hasty move; the letter my sister Kathy wrote from Kentucky as she learned to cook squirrel and was deciding not to marry the man who shot it; *The Child's Garden of Verses* that Mother illuminated with water colors while she read it to my brother and me, which my sister-in-law took; my father's old record of "St. James Infirmary," no longer playable. I regularly go back to the cupboard where I last saw one of the many slugs that my father made for me in his print shop. It was a shiny casting of printer's lead that I could press onto a stamp pad, then on paper to print a name. The first one said *Nancy*, my childhood name; a later one read *Clark*, because he made it for my son. The slug was always done in a cursive font, such as this: *Monotype Corsiva*, sometimes used for headlines. *Nancy* is not there.

These amassed materials open a window to my father. Tangible items like old 78 records tingle my memory, and letters and clippings fill in gaps to help me understand the boy and the man he was before I came along and started noticing things for myself. In among a daughter's discarded dresses, I keep some of the bound volumes of his weekly paper, the *Grays Harbor Post*, and microfilm of the rest. Of course, there's an old, awkward microfilm reader on a shelf above them, the better to look at my family's hard-to-focus past.

One day I typed up a formal chronology of my father's days on earth; my own life enters the list at his quarter-century mark. His breakdown makes a dark mark twenty years later. He and I coexist on the page for thirty-three years. The lineup of family events, births and marriages continues onto several new pages. On the hundredth anniversary of his birth, I got news of the arrival of his eighteenth great-grandchild.

I'm a writer, a retired teacher and software engineer, a wife and mother, a grandmother. I am also the daughter of that loving but melancholy printer who inherited a small print shop based on old technology, operating in a town in decline. A daughter trying to understand her ambivalent feelings toward that father.

I want to tell you how he lived. And died.

Kearny Clark's set of Printing Lessons

The story begins in the 1950s: setting type

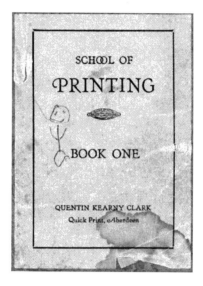

SCHOOL OF

PRINTING

BOOK ONE

QUENTIN KEARNY CLARK
Quick Print, Aberdeen

This book is an act of contrition for my wrongs
against my father. Working through the story
is my penance.

Kearny Clark at the Continental Divide, 1953

cA Trip Gone Wrong

Alexander MacDonald maintained and operated a toll road across this pass from 1876 to 1885... Water from the meadow lake flows to both the Pacific and the Atlantic Oceans.

—Marker at the Continental Divide, Montana

As conservators, my mother and I worked in tandem in the business of saving things. She gathered and stored souvenirs and maps from trips into neat packages, as I still do. There, in one of those shipped boxes, was a bunch of papers tied with grocery string, records from a driving trip during one of my college summers—gas station receipts, 2" x 2" snapshots, and the water-damaged spiral notebook travel diary. On the first page of the notebook, my younger handwriting offered a title, "The Big Push." I am flooded with memories of a trip gone wrong.

ॐ

The small blue Plymouth station wagon is headed out of town. My father is at the wheel, Mother, our eagle-eyed observer, sits beside him with an index finger fixing our place on the map, eager to point out curiosities and to watch for road signs. We are wound up, excited, anticipating a time-honored American auto-tourists' trek across the country. We're starting from Aberdeen, a lumber seaport in western Washington State. I am in the backseat plumping up a pillow and organizing the trip notebook. "Aug 1, 1953 and 3,000 miles to go." At almost twenty, I have two years of college behind me and hopes for two more.

Our destination is New York and my brother's graduation from the Merchant Marine Academy on Long Island. We left my two little sisters behind with Aunt Peggy. My father has taken time off from work—his first vacation since before the war, since he has been doing the work of two men in the family print shop.

Sixty miles from home we turn onto the new road south of Mount Rainier, and it feels like the trip has begun. White Pass has been open just two years; the road cuts are still raw, and there are no picnic areas. At a wide spot just over the four-thousand-foot pass, we stop to eat sandwiches. Mother opens the top of the Rollei camera, focuses. We smile in the mottled shade of tall firs, a father and daughter on a road trip.

After a stop for a fresh peach and a Schlitz, my father hands me the keys. Sometime later he writes in the journal, "Nance takes the throttle." The road toward Spokane twists through a narrow canyon with a river cascading far below us. I enjoy steering the car carefully on the winding road, leaning into each curve. His hand shakes as he tries to light his pipe, and he says, "Do you ever think you might drive right off the edge? Like the void's going to pull you into it?"

I don't know what to say. A cold fear grabs my heart. I don't like edges. Looking over a railing at the top of a tall building brings on a sudden lunge in the gut, weak knees. The sensation of blood plunging into my legs and feet rivet me to whatever I'm standing on. I grip the wheel more firmly. Nothing here is going to pull me off the road. I wonder what he is feeling? And why?

ॐ

Once at age four I was showing off, walking around on the wrong side of the railing above the steep stairway to my uncle Jack's basement, saying, *Look what I can do!* I remember the shock of wonder as I felt myself let go of the railing, the sickening blast of color in my head when I landed on the cement far below. I came to on the lawn and saw my father bent over me, his face anxious. He feared I would die. Someone said, "Don't turn her head, it might kill her."

ॐ

Driving after dark another day, as we try to eat up some miles, my father asks whether I see the huge coronas swirling around the street lights. I don't.

In Superior, Montana, after picnicking by the Clark River, we park and leave him in the passenger seat, while Mother and I go to a drug store and post office. He'd said he didn't feel like walking. When we come back we see that he has rifled the glove compartment and scattered things onto the bench seat: pipe tobacco, a tin of Band Aids, a tire gauge, some sandy shells, a scratchpad. Static crackles from the radio. He has taped a Band Aid over the glove box, as if to seal it, and is talking to himself. He keeps looking in the rear-view mirror. He cradles a folded newspaper with two hands, as if hiding a secret treasure, or a gun. Mother comes up beside him and asks him what he's doing. "Er, nothing, just looking for a match," he says, and lets the newspaper fall open to reveal a screwdriver. He empties his unlit pipe into the ashtray.

Mother drives the rest of the day.

ই

Just before the trip, my father hired me to help out at the shop. I filled in for some of the office people as they took their vacations—tasks ranging from writing society notes to picking up ad copy to bindery work. Our business occupied several large rooms above Pinckney Plumbing. My father employed as many as ten workers, and turned out quality job printing. Though nominally the manager, my father worked wherever he was needed, as a printer, pressman, or most often, linotypist. I enjoyed my brief stint at the shop but was eager to go back to college in the fall.

ই

Sagebrush alternating with shrubs and willows crowd the roadside. Mother, at the wheel, fingers another cigarette and pushes in the lighter. As she smokes she will try to distract my attention from what's becomes a steady stream of my father's odd behaviors: he won't look us in the eye; he keeps peering out the back window or the side mirror. Mother draws me out, "Tell me about your new friend Jean," or finds something in the passing scene: "Look at that hillside, those fluffy sheep! Have you ever seen so many?" My father does not join in our conversations. If he is mumbling in the back seat, we don't hear it over the noise of the road.

We don't talk about him. An unspoken understanding is building— this will be *our* secret. When it is my turn to drive, I ponder what must be happening to him, and a new memory hovers in the background:

It happened the summer we went camping at a beach or a river every weekend. I was four, almost five. We'd walked from the cars to the edge of a wide stream. Branches of a huge maple arched over the slow-moving, shallow water. People ahead of me had crossed to the other side on a wooden path and disappeared from view. My turn came to cross, and I balanced on the boards happily, looking for tadpoles, watching the riffles in the water, the pattern of rocks on the stream bottom.

Someone shouted, sounding excited and upset. It sounded like my mother's friend, Fran O'Connor. "Somebody help Kearny!"

I didn't see him fall. I didn't hear anything else. But the scream sent shivers through me. Something bad had happened to my father. Sunlight filtered through green leaves, and their shimmering reflections danced over the smooth flat stones of the stream's edge, engraving the green image into my mind. Low branches overhead offered shelter, planks bridging to the other shore, and gravel sloping upward opened to something unknown. The rush of water under the boards, the only sound. I felt alone, desolate.

That is the memory—my Green Tunnel Memory. No one told me what happened, neither to reassure me that all was well, nor to brush it off as "Nothing." I didn't hear the word *seizure* until years later. The adults must have hoped the kids hadn't noticed. The camping weekend continued as planned. A snapshot from that trip caught me, a skinny kid standing in shallow water eating a slice of watermelon, a bathing suit strap falling off one shoulder, hair escaped from a pigtail blown across my face, and several young aunts wading in the background. I seemed content to be there.

But the solidity of one of the pillars of my life felt threatened, a hairline crack insinuated in the construct of father.

☙

The modest auto courts where we stop are close to the highway and often also to the railroad tracks. Train whistles, thundering engines, and the rhythmic click-clack of the heavy rolling stock punctuate our dreams, but my father doesn't seem to mind. We'd heard how he watched the trains on his 1929 road trip, before he married. Being on the road means being close to trains. He seems on edge much of the time, causing me to wonder if he wishes he could hop on one and ride away.

I am the cheery daughter singing in the bathroom, daydreaming in the backseat, or all business when it is my turn to drive. The driving—my mother and I have taken over— feels like an impossible, interminable chore. It is hot; the only relief is a breeze coming in from a turned-in wind wing. As we make our way into the humid Midwest, I hate the feeling of the rayon slip and cotton dirndl sticking to the leatherette car seat, and to my legs.

My father tries to look normal, but he isn't making sense. He is nervous; he talks with his pipe clenched between his teeth; he doesn't know what to do with his hands. He says he is being followed, but doesn't know by whom or why. Mother seems to know how to handle him, telling him each time we get back in the car: "You'll be comfortable in the backseat. You can rest and read the paper." He does not complain. Posing for a snapshot, he looks slightly off-kilter, his cap askew, his body leaning against something.

We drive and drive on what seems like an eternity of concrete ribbons and through hundreds of small towns. Belching trucks loom in the rear-view mirror on the downhills, threatening to push us out of the way, then hold us back on the next uphill grade. This is 1953, our new president, Eisenhower, has not yet set the country to work on interstate highways. Between us and New York are miles and miles of narrow two-lane roads whose construction barely disturbed the contours of the land. I have plenty of time to worry.

It seems that my father's mind is making the transition I saw in art history paintings: serene landscapes morphing into tortured, terrifying places where every tree, cloud, or star is surrounded by a brashly swirling corona, by threatening waves of light and dark. I know Van Gogh was a sick man. I don't know what is wrong with my father. What he is seeing or feeling scares him.

౿

Mother and I take turns making meticulous entries in our journal about mileage, gas, and other purchases, but never once do we write anything about the change in my father. We record each lost hour crossing into a new time zone, a supper in Billings where Daddy scrawls, "Lost hat," the sighting of several oil wells, watching sport fishermen ("No hat"), lunch in a new cemetery (Mother: "Nobody's planted yet!"). We write nothing about what we are feeling, the desperate sense that with just two of us driving we might never get to Wisconsin, never mind all the states beyond Lake Michigan!

My father has moments of lucidity and gets into the spirit of journaling. On the fourth day out he writes: "2 pm–lunch in a wheatfield out of Dickinson, N.D. Some doubt whether Nance or Mama inspired the wolf calls, whistles." What would he think if he saw a note on the page, if Mother were to write, "Kearny acting strange," or I were to pen, "What's wrong with Daddy?"

౿

My own world beckons. I have boyfriends to ponder. When it's my turn in the backseat I daydream about my future, the endless time that stretches out beyond. I see myself as a grown up woman wearing pretty clothes. She's holding the hand of a child, other children in Sunday clothes trail behind her like a clutch of ducklings, always walking along some unfamiliar sidewalk in a nice neighborhood. I know I want a husband, but my late-blooming body is only beginning to be aware of what is interesting and attracting about a man.

Because of what I'm seeing so close at hand, I am realizing that the "right man" must not be like my father. The center-fielder with the electric blue eyes whom I dated back at school is too much like him: too focused on his batting slump, too melancholy to relate to other people. Tom doesn't like parties, he doesn't like my friends, he doesn't much like himself. I want someone exciting, outgoing, agreeably cheerful, considerate, and smart.

੬

Since my father publishes a weekly paper, I am used to seeing our names in its pages. The society editor will report on this trip in the *Social and Society News Notes* on page two. Many events in my life, such as birthday parties, teas I hosted, have been cast in metal slugs and pressed onto shiny book stock, bound into the year's volume. My past is tidy, safe.

Though I didn't read them until years later, my father's editorials during the Truman years analyzed subjects that don't seem to go away. He criticized the new United Nations, the policies of our State Department, and of our U.N. ambassador, Eleanor Roosevelt. In the midst of the Korean Conflict the previous spring, President Truman fired General MacArthur— my senior English class listened to the general's famous "Old Soldiers Never Die" speech. My father called the firing, "the summary action of an erratic and unpredictable administration." The next week he questioned the wisdom of having the president be commander-in-chief, asking "what is the world coming to when a [former] artillery captain is in a position to fire a five-star general?" He needn't worry that such an affront would happen again, since former General "Ike" Eisenhower had moved into the White House. (MacArthur outranked Eisenhower by mere days, it would have been interesting.)

੬

At dinner in Bismarck my father stares at his plate as if he's never seen chicken-fried steak and mashed potatoes before. He smells the food as if it were poisoned and pushes bites around with his fork and only reluctantly eats some of it. The next morning I stare out the car window at the barren Dakota grassland and flirt with a new worry: how will this man who seems to be losing his mind be able to write a coherent opinion piece when we get home? How will he keep the business going?

There is little time to read the book my father brought along for me: *Inside USA* by John Gunther. Probably a review copy from the publisher, it is thick, more than nine hundred pages of fine print. I like the idea of it; the author traveled to every state and wrote about the people and the politicians. Wouldn't it be interesting to read about life in the country we are crossing? Gunther is a reporter. That's how I think of myself sometimes, though I am majoring in elementary education rather than journalism. He must have driven many of these same, slow, roads.

We are following the northern route, mostly U.S. Highway 10 and sometimes 12, that winds through Montana, North Dakota, and Minnesota. We notice the different character of Midwest deciduous forests, admire scatterings of conical evergreens that make me think of scenes on summer cottage wallpaper. We each at one time or another say, "These people don't know what a real forest looks like," homesick already for the enormous firs and cedars of our Northwest rain forests.

Boarding a night ferry to cross Lake Michigan brings a nice change of pace, the freedom of being on open water, fresh air, and someone else at the wheel. On such a big boat I hope I can get away from my parents for a while.

As the lights of Milwaukee grow tiny, my father seems cheerful, actually smiling for a few minutes; then he tenses, whispers, "Don't look now, over there..." and points to two men in suits further down the railing of the Clipper. They look like business men, but we move away. Later we go below to find seats for the long ride and my father starts talking to a man nearby, the fear forgotten. He boasts that he is traveling with two of the most amazing women you would ever meet. He goes on and on about how wonderful we are, what a great mother his wife is, until the beleaguered listener excuses himself and finds another seat. My father's strange talkativeness is embarrassing. He feels he's being watched one minute, and reaches out to strangers the next. Weird. I don't want to be seen with him.

Even though we've been behind schedule the whole trip, my parents have taken time to sit down for a beer most days. I'm still underage. Sitting with my book outside the bar or tavern I recall long slow hours during the war, when my brother and I waited in the back seat of our car while Mother tried to get Daddy out of the Bright Spot tavern after work. Plaintive phrases run through my head: "Father, dear Father, come home with me now," or "What's keeping dear Father, why doesn't he come?" These are songs my mother played for us from her mother's green volumes of the *Old Home Music Library*, music I loved. My father loves beer and hard liquor and won't be hurried. Perhaps the drinking helps him lose his pursuers, or silences whatever is going on in his head.

❦

Partway across Michigan we stop at a pay phone to call my brother with a progress report. I hear Mother's side of the conversation:

"Yes, Michigan. We're almost to Lansing."

"Yes, late. We're doing our best."

"Yes. How much do you need?"

❦

We maneuver the streets of Detroit and its bridges and start across rural southern Ontario, the "Sun Parlor" of Canada, and I think about the brother we will soon see:

Phil. Of course I worship him; he's my big brother. He has a confidence that makes you want him on your team, a smile you want to trigger, a smugness you envy. I knew from childhood that he had the dash and swagger that my father lacked, that *his* brother, our uncle Jack, had. Phil took to the outdoors like our Clark grandfather. Barely five, he would sneak out before sunrise to go fishing in the gully below our house and come home with a good-sized minnow. He brought home stray dogs, frogs, salamanders, and nearly dead kittens. He and a friend backpacked in the wild North River country south of Grays Harbor. He thought nothing of sleeping in a gravel pit on a weekend jaunt out of town.

I am glad we will be seeing him soon. We return to the United States near Niagara Falls to reach our first objective, Aunt Louise's in Tonawanda, a suburb of Buffalo, late on August 7. Mother's oldest sister, Louise, is always homesick for news of the Northwest, and is glad to see us.

"You poor things," she says. "You need a rest." Since we've driven more than 2,700 miles, we let her talk us into a day off. Mother wires fifty dollars to Phil, we pack a picnic lunch and go to gape at Niagara Falls. Our journal will summarize our eventual accomplishment: 7,478 miles in twenty-eight days, spending $960.00. In those days gasoline cost 36 cents a gallon, dinners for three or four, our only restaurant meal, seldom more than $7.50. Heading east again the next morning, we are two days behind schedule.

We pass through "Italian parts of Albany and on down to Taconic State Parkway and direct to Danbury," where we spend the night. Heading south from there, finding no parkways, we get truly lost in the winding, overgrown roads of the New York City reservoir system. We barely arrive in Kings Point, just across the Wheatstone Bridge on Long Island, on my birthday, August 10, in time to change for the graduation ceremony. My father, distinctly uncomfortable in a suit and tie, stays close to Mother. Phil looks smashing, straight and tall and handsome in his dress whites, his officer's cap. My father is proud of him. Here is another person on whom he can dish lavish praise. We say nothing to my brother about what is going on with his father. He will see for himself soon enough.

౽

Phil will drive home with us for a leave, but has things to finish up. My parents and I spend a few days sightseeing in New York City. We take a boat ride around Manhattan Island and go to see the Dodgers play the Giants at the Polo Grounds; Daddy is pleased because "the Bums" won! One memory from that visit stands out.

We are walking downtown on the Avenue of the Americas. My mother and I are talking about the murals we've just seen in Rockefeller Center and about what else we hoped to see while we are in the city. The energy of a Manhattan street is contagious, and we are walking fast, as if we've some-where to go.

Then we realize we've gotten ahead of my father. Or perhaps lost him. We look back, but he is not in sight. We step to the curb to let others pass. Many well-dressed people hurry by, as well as some gawkers, tourists like us, unused to so many tall buildings, so much noisy traffic.

Small knots of men loiter beside shop entrances, several are leaning against a blank wall. Their clothes are dark, even their hats are dark, their faces indistinguishable. Then one of the figures takes a stick match out of a shirt pocket, whips it along the underside of a trousered leg, cups the flame to the bowl of a pipe, and pulls on it to get a red glow.

We have found Daddy.

He is trying to disappear. His hat is pulled down so no one will recognize him. As he puffs on his pipe, he strikes up a conversation with the man next to him, in the overly friendly manner that seems to have overtaken him.

He steps away from the wall and grudgingly agrees to stay closer to us. We start walking again and find we'll have to slow down. He will walk with us, but at his own speed, continually drifting two or three paces behind, like a reluctant child headed for the dentist's office.

I am embarrassed to see him looking so out of place, his clothes hanging carelessly, his steps uncertain as he straggles behind. He is acting like a tramp, and seems pretty happy about it.

Why can't he be like my friend Ann's father, so good looking and neatly dressed, who comes to church with his family even though he is always bored. After Mass he tells us how many candles had been lighted, the number of cracks in the plaster, the number of times Father O'Donnell said "Umm" during the sermon.

The comparison, of course, is not fair. Ann's father is one of our town's lumber barons who married the daughter of another—he can choose not to work if he wants to; my father is a printer who inherited too much responsibility when he was the one left to run the business.

I don't understand what has happened to him on this trip. We will call it a "nervous breakdown" in the next few years, but I don't know that yet. I am already extending the case against him, collecting the observations that will allow me to reject him. I do not want the tramp-like man I see behind me on that Manhattan sidewalk to be my father.

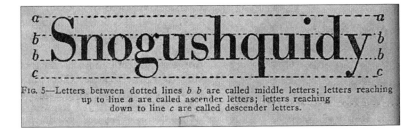

FIG. 5—Letters between dotted lines *b b* are called middle letters; letters reaching up to line *a* are called ascender letters; letters reaching down to line *c* are called descender letters.

A curious word in a Printing Lesson
created to illustrate letter lore

My Brief Career as a Bindery Girl

Help Wanted: Casual employment as a bindery worker in a print shop. Finishing tasks such as folding, numbering, assembling, stapling, counting, bundling, and wrapping printing jobs for delivery. Familiarity with standard proofreaders' marks helpful. Only relatives of the boss need apply.

— Kearny Clark

Fresh off the train from California after my sophomore year of college, but before the Trip Gone Wrong, I sat on Mother's perch in the kitchen and admired her organizational skills. She'd punched holes in the edge of my letters and filed them in a black three-ring binder along with those of my brother from Kingspoint.

The binder stood beside the flour canister on the kitchen counter— salt, sugar, flour, letters from progeny. Tiny school pennant stickers marked the battered spine of the notebook, one for each of our schools—Stanford and the United States Merchant Marine Academy. The notebook survived in a dusty box for forty years in my mother's archive, and the contents are still in good shape, the paper only slightly yellowed. I scarcely remember being the excited girl who wrote those breathless missives, a girl who often wrote in the third person:

Branner Hall, 1951-53

> *Dear family,*
>
> *Your eldest daughter at long last takes pen in hand to tell you of her life at Stanford...* She, this eldest daughter, is out for fun and says so. She describes dates, organizations joined, praises everything about the place and assures her parents that the school is making sure the students know they are special.

She doesn't mention her growing realization that she is no longer the smartest kid in the class, especially in a special Western Civ section—along with other valedictorians from bigger high schools—taught, not by an instructor, but by the head of the program, distinguished Professor William Bark. Humbling!

She sprinkles ungrammatical expressions into her letters in the folksy style affected by her father, presumably to help him relate to her letters, to bring him in. *(It's time to close this-here epistle.)* She intersperses newly acquired French phrases, most of them from *Le Petit Prince*, because she knows her mother studied French in high school. *(On ne sait jamais.)* One never knows.

She raves about her roommates, her friends, she decorates her dorm room, she enjoys the food. Until the rains come in January, she doesn't mention the sunshine, knowing the folks at home aren't seeing any. She talks about the football games, sounding like she really pays attention, knowing her readers care.

She always apologizes for not writing sooner, or more often. Humble apologies. Every letter. So does her brother.

Her more studious friends label her a *rah rah*. She gets picked for Rally Committee, a lot of work, but is it ever fun! She gets to be a cheerleader! At the Rose Bowl her team loses to Illinois. *It really was a thrill to lead that monstrous student body in the songs, though, in that beautiful full bowl, jammed with people…wow!*

She types the letters unless her roommates are sleeping. She wears out several typewriter ribbons, but never runs out of exclamation points. Mid-freshman year she gets the job as a hasher and waitress in the dining hall. This covers board, and she makes friends with the male hashers, many of whom are athletes.

She works hard to get a scholarship for the second year, then fritters away her concentration that year on activities and social life. She wins a campus-wide election for secretary of the Association of Women Students, defeating, among others, the classmate who goes on to be a long-term senator from California. On an almost-failed French exam, her Professor writes, *"Too much extra-curricular, perhaps, Mademoiselle?"*

In the spring of her sophomore year her letters describe hours sitting in the sunny baseball stadium. Her fellow hasher with the ice blue eyes plays centerfield. What she does not describe are hours spent in his Model A Ford in the dining hall parking lot, while her class work suffers.

For now, I am,

> *Your loving eldest daughter,*
> *Nancy*

ॐ

We expected to make what we would call "The Big Push" to New York in August but meanwhile that young Nancy would qualify for the position at the shop as a bindery worker.

I even agreed to take over the front office for two weeks while the office girl, Emmy, went on vacation. The summer plan was complicated. My father and I would hold the fort at home while Mother and the little girls moved to the rented house, called The Barn, at the beach. Mother's sister Peggy would come there to tend the girls so that my parents and I could be gone for most of the month of August. Until then, we working folks, like big city types, would spend the week at our jobs and drive out to Cohassett Beach to join the vacationing family on weekends— all 24 miles.

ॐ

When my grandfather ran the print shop, the front office looked more like a hunting lodge than a newspaper office. To make sure posterity would know of his prowess in the outdoors he called in B.B. Jones and sat for a photograph. The Boss in a dark vest, pinstripes, shirt sleeves, and tie sits in a swivel chair at a sturdy table beside his cluttered roll top desk. Books and stacks of papers crowd the table's surface. A panoramic photo of Grays Harbor in 1910 and a large framed portrait of his youngest son, my father, a toddler in a knitted snowsuit holding a tin horn and standing on a Victorian carved chair, attest to his love of town and family. The door to the rest of the print shop and his stenographer's work area is blocked by a stuffed Roosevelt elk.

In life, that half-ton creature roamed the Olympic Mountains; its species had been named in honor of President Theodore Roosevelt. My grandfather, The Great White Hunter, shot it, and kept it, I'm sure, to impress his friends and to commemorate a successful trip into the woods he loved. How did the taxidermist get it there? In its preserved magnificence, its antlers rose at least a foot and a half above the doorway, and its substantial body filled an entire third of the room. A spittoon stood at hand near the elk's hind legs. J.W. Clark, his desks, and two wooden chairs took up the rest.

ॐ

By the time my father took charge of the shop, the elk had found a home in the lobby of the Elk's Club and the front office had become female territory. Three large wooden office desks filled the room, one for the office girl, one for the society editor or any other part-timer, and a third for the occasional news man. A sturdy black Diebold safe, with a pastoral scene that split in half when the heavy doors opened, stood against the west wall that for years had seen the rump of the elk.

The office girl served as stenographer and girl-Friday, with her finger on the pulse of Quick Print Co. She answered the phone and used a jerry-built intercom to notify men in the back shop of phone calls or messages, she proofread all copy, collected time sheets, typed invoices, handled the mail, balanced the bank account, and more. She added a welcomed female presence to a holiday party in the back shop.

I recall an Amy, a Gertie, a Maggie. This summer it was Emmy Laaksonen who would mentor me through the weeks. I loved to hear her talk to her grandmother in noon-time telephone conversations—the stream of Finnish language a lilting and melodic delight.

The only office space my father claimed for himself had been carved out of the bindery room between the office and the back shop. A flimsy partition along the window wall created two compartments the depth of the roll-top desk, an area everyone called the "Hell-Hole." One compartment was my father's, the other was available for the sports writer.

My father's sleek two-toned green Corona portable typewriter with a green ribbon usually sat on a small table next to the desk in his compartment. Over the years he typed out editorials, obituaries, letters, and wills on his trusty machine. This was the same machine I had set on our ping pong table in order to teach myself to type, pecking out several acts by Shakespeare: "But soft! What light through yonder window breaks?" and "Romeo! Wherefore art thou Romeo?" Alas, it is now an aging artifact in my family archive, having succumbed to a broken carriage-cable. Where would I find parts for an eighty-year-old typewriter?

Friday mornings, my father put on the old green eyeshade and took his seat at the Linotype keyboard. If he had not thumped out his editorial at the kitchen table the night before, he wrote it there and then. The galley of slugs would still be warm as he or Uncle Alec locked it into the frame while composing the editorial page.

❧

Images of that early summer linger in my memory: my father at the kitchen table reading the paper, a drink at his side; I at the stove cooking something so we don't starve—broiled salmon steaks, slices of tomato, buttered toast. Kraft macaroni and cheese. I haven't cooked much. Cakes and cookies are the sum of my culinary experience. And at the shop: my father at his typecasting machines: the Linotype and the Ludlow, trimming cuts from the stereotype on the metal saw, leaning against a type case loading tobacco into his pipe, chewing the fat with the Hammermill paper salesman, smiling.

There'd been no reason to pay special attention to him. Who anticipates that a vacation road trip would become a life-changing event? I hadn't questioned my father's sanity. I had not said to myself, watch what he's doing, he might never be able to pick up a composing stick again. I'd no inkling that I should be noticing and remembering anything. After all, he was a forty-five-year-old man with a wife and four children, a printer managing a small print shop, the father I'd grown up with, no more, no less.

Even so, things did feel upside down that summer. Our house, where I'd been the pampered eldest daughter, was now my responsibility–the laundry, the yard, as well as the meals. Though I'd done some useful work at the shop, it had always seemed like an extension of family and a playground. Now it was a serious workplace. Though just a college girl home for the summer, with friends to see, I had a job.

My father and I mimicked the bachelor household that had once flourished in the big house below ours. In my grandfather's day, he, his sister-in-law, Klara, and his two adult sons sat together at meals, then each drove his or her own car downtown to the same workplace. One big difference from grandfather's household—my father never hired a cook. But we did have plenty of cars. The shop's delivery car—a sorry two-door affair with no backseat—was balky and hard to drive. Aunt Klara's prewar Chrysler sedan, one of the first cars with fluid drive, was now ours. And we still had the convertible, but Mother had gone to the beach in the sensible Plymouth wagon that we would drive to New York.

❦

One week, that summer of '53, I camped at the "society desk," doing small folding and collating jobs and writing articles for the society page of the *Post*. Pages two and three featured brief notices about the parties, travels, visitors, and weddings of people known to the woman who collected the information. For years, my namesake, my father's Aunt Klara, held this position. She wrote about the doings of her golfing friends, our family, and many women's clubs. For wedding stories, she collected detailed information about the bride, the groom, the bride's gown, her flowers, her going-away suit, the mother of the bride's outfit, the attendants and their attire, the couple's backgrounds. She couldn't possibly have attended all of these weddings, so the printers teased her when she wrote, "The bride looked beautiful in ivory satin" or "... Chinese silk," or some other luxurious-sounding fabric, whatever had been filled in on the wedding form she'd created. She was gone by the time my wedding announcement appeared in the paper, and the account lacked descriptive details because I wasn't asked to fill out the form. Aunt Klara could not have imagined her grandniece looking beautiful in a simple sheath of faux white linen.

❧

The paperless world, much touted as a boon of the computer revolution, eludes me today in my home office. Or rather, I reject it, printing out emails and photos and articles and stashing them somewhere. Digital images of family members festoon the walls of my office. Heaps of notes, drafts, and unfinished manuscripts offer shifting nap sites for my cats. Untidy folders lean in the bookshelves, a pile of catalogues lies on the floor under the large *Webster's* Third. Random papers overflow several in-boxes, books and papers rest crossways over many shelved books.

I come by this love of paper clutter honestly. It started back in the stockroom of the print shop, where every surface sagged under the weight of stacks of paper, where as a child I was never told, "Don't touch." Odds and ends in the shop's waste baskets became my raw materials for making fancy dolls, sometimes decked out in a skirt of red or gold paper. I would crawl onto a package of paper in one of the cubbies, stretch out full length like a cat relaxing soft-side up on a cushion and peek out of the shelf. The long narrow room was lined all the way around with columns of shelves, some of them small, some large like this one. Out of almost every cubby hole where someone had opened a package, torn wrappings waved at odd angles like pennants at a football game. Light came in from a skylight and from a single bulb hanging in the middle of the room. I'd inhale the clean smell of paper and imagine I was the picture printed on a huge page. This was my fortress.

❧

How did the huge bundles of paper make it out of a truck, up the double stairway and into the shelves? They were bulky and hard to handle. I'd never seen a delivery, but I did know how big sheets turned into small ones.

The paper cutting machine, a monstrous mass of cast metal with smooth calibrated surfaces, levers, cranks, and wheels, could easily accommodate a thick stack of the largest paper in the opening below the electrically powered guillotine cutter. The sharp, shiny blade was barely visible in the superstructure. I loved to follow Uncle Alec—an in-law on my mother's side—as he brought a bundle of paper from the stockroom and flung it like a heavy blanket onto the bed of the cutter, smoothed it out and nestled it against the stops at the back. His hands would be everywhere under the blade as he cranked the bed forward or back to set the depth for the first cut. He reached up and turned a large horizontal wheel to bring the paper holder down tight, securing the stack. I watched with open-mouthed concentration. What if he pinched his fingers, what if the blade cut one off?

He'd straighten up, push me out of the way, and pull a big handle sideways. The wide vertical blade sliced diagonally across the firmly held stack, then retreated into home position. The cutting motion made a loud "ss-sl-lk-k" in a descending scale, and it sent a shock wave through my body, like the sensation that comes from even thinking about a razor blade coming near skin. Again his hands moved in under the blade. He'd remove the outside stack, or maybe add it to the one just cut, reach under the knife to rotate the cut stack, adjust his crank, and repeat the process. My heart raced faster knowing he was going to pull that handle again, another slice. The cut face was often perfectly smooth like a slab of butter, but sometimes showed a moiré pattern due to variations in the paper or the knife edge. In the hands of a skilled operator, the cutter turned huge pieces of paper into neat stacks of custom-ordered invoice-sized sheets, a process repeated for three or four colors. On a final trim cut, a cascade of long skinny strips fell away from the shiny blade, fodder for the trash barrel, and welcome supplies for my doll-making.

ॐ

Several afternoons that summer of '53 I held copy for Emmy who had refreshed me on the list of proofreader's marks. Reading copy is an exercise in speaking clearly and enunciating with precision every typographic or punctuation mark. She read quickly and I hoped to hear some of the music of the conversations with her grandmother as I frantically marked typos or deletions.

Some tasks felt like make-work: drive out to the coast to pick up copy from one or two correspondents. I'd stop for coffee at the Westhaven dock, pretending to be a reporter listening for news, and watch fishermen unload fresh tuna and salmon from their well-iced holds, a chance to buy fresh salmon steaks or cracked crab. In town I also delivered jobs wrapped earlier, and picked up ads from local stores to be set for the week's paper.

෴

When I tell someone my family had its own newspaper, it feels like putting on airs, asserting how different, how important we were. Oh! A newspaper! Watch for reflected awe. I hoped my listener was visualizing some version of the *New York Times* with its angular nameplate and many pages of up-to-date and important stories about what is going on in the wide world. Or something like the now-abbreviated *Salt Lake Tribune*, which publishes some national and plenty of local news. But if you think of folksy articles in the vein of the "News from Lake Wobegon," you're getting closer to the mark.

A large newspaper establishment would have specialists responsible for each function: reporters and editors to create content, typesetters and layout men, printers and pressmen to assure the appearance of the final product. And proofreaders. In my father's modest operation for the *Grays Harbor Post*, the editor often wore two hats, or brought all of them together under the green eyeshade: publisher, reporter, editorial writer, typesetter and printer. In a pinch he could run the press.

The *Post* went out in Saturday's mail, a slim eight-page deal. Well past being fresh, the "news" had already appeared in the local daily and been read over local radio by the reporter who threw his packet of articles and stories over the transom in the hall door on Thursday nights to be set for Friday's press run.

These many years later, I inflate the stature of the paper, imagining its name set in the elaborate European-looking font the *New York Times* uses, something like Old English. On checking, I am disappointed to see that the *Post*'s nameplate was presented in a fat, upright font called **Poster Bodoni:**

Grays Harbor Post

The paper came out weekly, mailed to possibly a thousand subscribers. I don't believe anyone sent out past-due notices. Subscription renewals resembled church contributions: sporadic and voluntary. If you were a friend of the family, a local business, an advertiser, your name was on the list, and your postman brought your *Post* every Saturday morning.

On Friday afternoon, my job was to get mailing labels onto the finished papers. I wound the long paper tape of subscribers' names and addresses into the contraption that would attach them onto the paper. The labeler was awkward, big as a breadbox, with a handle, a cutting blade, and a roller in a glue reservoir. The wheat paste glue mustn't be lumpy, and not too runny, a just-right smelly but useful porridge. The heavy machine worked smoothly most of the time. The windowless bindery area felt muggy, uncomfortable that afternoon. The machine and I pounded out label after label, then the tape would break, or the glue reservoir would run dry, or my arm would tire, or...I looked forward to Emmy's return.

The print run wasn't as large as a thousand by that time, or I never would have gotten through it. My father bundled the stacks of labeled papers into canvas mail baskets and hefted them off to the post office two blocks up the street. He and the shop crew disappeared into the Bright Spot, and I drove out to join the family at the beach.

࿇

In the bindery area, I found myself surrounded by jobs I would learn to do with dexterity that summer: multicolored stacks of numbered business forms to be collated, finished jobs to be wrapped with neat printer's corners like reams of paper, booklets to be stapled. Overhead, flimsy shelves sagged under years' worth of file copies of the *Post*. From the back shop around the corner I heard the clack of the linotype, the regular whine of a printing press, inhaled a mixture of hot lead and ink and scorched paper and knew this was a welcoming, familiar place. We Clarks often claimed that we had printers' ink in our veins and standard proofreaders' marks embedded in our vocabulary. I can't read a block of text or a menu or a playbill without seeing typos. Modern copy machines now incorporate many of the bindery chores I mastered, rendering bindery workers—not to mention printers and typesetters—obsolete.

࿇

The stockroom where I had once made paper dolls by then had the only worktable where we could number ballots: stacks of old-fashioned paper ballots for each voting precinct, each with a tiny perforated corner that had to bear a unique number on its backside. Because of the B.B. Jones photograph, I recognize the table as my grandfather's former desk from the front office. While still in high school, I sat with a group of college girls around the rickety table, our numbering machines in full motion. They talked about the local boys who had been sent to Korea with the first group of Marine reservists. The office girl's best friend hadn't heard from her fiancé, now on a battlefield. The news from Korea was all bad, our men were getting killed, they lamented, we were losing. The stockroom that had seemed safe and secure, a favorite playroom, suddenly felt drafty and mean. I began to notice the dirty glass in the skylight, the clutter on the shelves around us, the oil-stained floors. I felt helpless as I pounded numbers onto ballot corners, tidied up one precinct's ballots, reset the numbering machine, and picked up another. My fortress, no longer a shelter.

ॐ

Emmy turned her job over to me for the last two weeks of July 1953. I sat at her desk and pretended to be the office girl, hoping the phone wouldn't ring. I didn't dare open any desk drawer and had moments of panic—what if the men in the shop saw that I didn't know what I was doing?

She left me a list of tasks. I calculated invoices for the boilerplate from several national services. *Papier-mâché* mats arrived in the mail, our printers cast them in metal, cut the casting apart and used the cuts as filler in the newspaper: recipes, sewing patterns, house plans, human interest and celebrity photos; there were also advertising cuts. We billed so much per column inch for advertisements, for example for railroad, airline, cigarette or telephone companies and Lydia E. Pinkham ads for products to ease women's distress. I recall typing an invoice to Batten, Barton, Durstine and Osborn, because those were names thrown about as a joke by Jack Benny and other radio personalities; the history of the advertising company BBDO inspired the TV series, *Mad Men*.

It felt good to be useful, and I liked earning money. One day on an errand to pick up ad copy from the nearby men's store, I bought four yards of men's tweed fabric to make into a suit for myself. Another day I came back from a lunch time shopping trip with a pair of blue platform pumps I'd been pleased to buy for thirty dollars. A pressman stopped to chat, maybe it was Moody, and saw the package as I stuffed it into a cupboard outside the stockroom. When he started at the shop, he said, he earned thirty-five cents an hour. The shoes suddenly seemed extravagant, representing most of a week's wages at one dollar an hour. I didn't have to pay for food or rent, or even gas for the car I drove. Though the shoes matched my blue suit, they were never comfortable.

ॐ

My least favorite task was what Emmy did every lunch hour while eating at her desk: call each business on the Accounts Receivable list to find out when they were planning to pay their bill. It was a long list. I hadn't realized that a company didn't just cut a check when a dunning statement arrived. And my father's business might be such a company.

The *Post* depended on income from the county's legal notices and institutional ads from big companies, such as Weyerhaeuser, Rayonier, or Harbor Plywood, companies on the endangered list, at least on the Harbor. Local merchants were put off by the Saturday delivery of the paper—they'd have preferred a Wednesday or Thursday mailing in order to advertise weekend specials. I heard discussions about the advisability of change, but it didn't happen.

My father managed as best he could, trying to satisfy customer orders with old technology, meeting payroll without benefit of a salesman to bring in more work. Other printing plants in town were buying offset presses, which were cheaper to operate but didn't produce as crisp an image as letterpress printing. He preferred doing things as had his brother, his father. He didn't want to lower the quality of his job work or take risks on new equipment or a new format for the paper. Though I didn't realize it at the time, those early summer weeks at the shop marked the close of the secure chapters of our family saga, the chapters with my father in charge and able to provide for his family.

ॐ

As we packed the car for the drive east he'd been cheerful, joking with our neighbors who lent us their compact travel kitchen box, drinking toasts to each other and one for the road. Could the pressure to get away from the shop, the excited anticipation of a long vacation, the expectation of seeing the big city and his son, could all of this have caused his breakdown?

ॐ

The father who came back from the trip to New York seemed like another person, a confused and helpless man. I stopped paying attention to him. Convinced that she needed to do something, Mother contacted doctors and psychiatrists, looking for answers. Would he recover? What would happen at the shop? She could only hope that his employees would keep things going until he was able to go back to work.

September came. The family agreed I should go back to college. Their "sweet eldest daughter Nancy" would return to the campus where she had for two years answered only to "Klancy," the nickname given her by her Great White Hunter grandfather.

Mother did her best to keep up appearances at home. Only now, searching her archive, do I appreciate how difficult those years must have been. I'd taken for granted her ability to keep the house "shipshape" and able to support the activities of her children—she'd always followed through when one of us said, "My mom'll bake a chocolate cake." But my father's illness shook her world. She lost track of the letters I sent home during my last two college years, a notable lapse in her faithful husbanding of valued papers. Few as there may have been, those missives never made it into the black three-ring binder in the kitchen counter line-up: salt, sugar, flour, letters from progeny.

Kearny and little Nancy, 1938

Looking Back

Vanity and pride are different things, though the words are often used synonymously. A person may be proud without being vain. Pride relates more to our opinion of ourselves, vanity to what we would have others think of us.

— Jane Austen, *Pride and Prejudice*

A snapshot. It is one of the few photos of the four of us together, taken before the war, before little sisters, before my father became sick.

Cut off at the knees, I am backed up by my father, mother, and brother. We are standing in sepia uphill of the house where my mother grew up. We're all wearing warm clothes, but Mother's coat is luxuriant, a full-length, blousy-sleeved Persian lamb fur with a bouffant collar. Mother wrote "March 1938" on the back of the photo. I am four and a half and Phil is seven.

My still-blonde hair hangs out under a felt hat—I think it was red. I am standing in front of my father holding what looks like a sucker. Mother is restraining my brother, a frowning and whistling captive, looking like he will run away as soon as she lets go. My father is smiling and cradling the bowl of his pipe in his hand; his tie is a bit askew and the tips of his collar curl out. My right elbow is bent in the same way as my father's, my sucker in the same position as the stem of his pipe.

In the background our old Chrysler roadster with the six wire wheels and the rumble seat is parked in front of my grandfather's house.

This is the family of my childhood. A brother who teases me. A father who is a printer. A homemaker mother. We are beginning to enjoy some financial comfort. I will spend the summer on our lawn building castles out of the wooden shipping box from our first automatic washer, a Bendix. My father will soon trade in the roadster for a Chevy with two doors and a proper back seat. We are the foursome who will drive to the San Francisco World's Fair the next summer in the new car. We kids will make life miserable on that drive—Phil with his small bladder, I with a queasy stomach. My mother will save the day with a milk bottle for Phil and a dishpan for me. My father will fail to cajole a monkey at the San Diego Zoo into giving back a button from my favorite coat. Back home, we will camp every weekend in the coming two summers. We camp at every ocean beach and river park in the area, but never at the lake where my father's brother Perry drowned. On one of these camping trips, the sun filtering through a green tunnel of big leaf maples onto a rock-strewn stream is fixed indelibly into my mind.

We are the foursome bound by love, and in 1938 we think we are simply a happy family.

ॐ

My mother, Dorothy Nielsen Clark, was steady in the face of her husband's illness. It was merely another challenge among many: her own self-absorbed mother, the runaway boyfriend, the husband so silent during the war. She had a comfortable house and two daughters still at home. So far, the house and cars were unencumbered. If her husband was sick, she would find some way to make him well. Though she had seen a sister "give in" to mental illness, that wouldn't happen, not to her family, not to her husband.

Attractive, but never a beauty, she favored the guarded smile that hid her teeth, even after the miracle of perfect dentures. She was not vain, but appreciated her natural curl, as have her descendants who share the trait. She made friends easily.

She spoke in imperatives. Long before Nike, she was one to say, "Just do it." "Stop agonizing and go to school." I can only talk about her in simple declaratives. And in present tense, even though she's been gone for twenty-some years. Her fearless voice still echoes in my head.

Mother was not one to cry. She exuded security, confidence. Her lips were the only soft thing about her.

Dorothy had been her father's favorite. As soon as her father taught her to drive, he turned the Packard over to her on family outings. When in high school she and another Dorothy became great friends, she adopted her father's nickname, "Pete."

Observant and eager to enjoy life, her Silver Lining Detector was ever at the ready.

Growing up, Mother joined her older sisters in working to keep things on an even keel in the household while their mother, newly-converted to Catholicism, added more babies until there were nine.

Grandmother Rhoda had trained as a nurse and worked briefly before she married Peter Nielsen, a Danish-immigrant druggist. She seldom completed her *toilette* before noon and never arrived on time for anything. She was generous and emotional. The more capable Dorothy and her sisters became, the more work Grandmother Rhoda turned over to them. As her daughters matured and looked for mates, she ridiculed any suitor one might bring home. Dorothy kept her boyfriend to herself, and ultimately eloped.

❦

The give and take of marriage and child-raising sometimes required that Dorothy plumb the depths of her reservoir of calm, composure, competence, and coping skills. And somehow she managed to see the good in most of us.

I still hear her affirmations: "Everything is fine. We're managing. My children are wonderful. Doing fine and getting better." And, "Why focus on what you can't change. Let's go to the beach and cut a pine tree."

She was a reader. She read all the time. *The Seattle Post Intelligencer* accompanied her breakfast of coffee with sugar and cream skimmed off the top of the milk bottle. The evening's *Aberdeen Daily World* enlivened cocktail hour. Magazines like *Time, Saturday Evening Post,* or *Life* engaged her as she sat in her chair to the right of the fireplace. Stretching out on the couch after the housework was done, she devoured novels from the library, mysteries, the latest arrival from the Book-of-the-Month Club. She often reread her favorite book, *I Capture the Castle* by Dodie Smith. My sisters and I also reread it often, recognizing the heroine, Cassandra Mortmain and our mother as kindred spirits. Cassandra also was sensible, outgoing and a doer.

❦

Among my report cards from grade school, old postcards, and Mother's tinted eye glasses, I find a familiar scene from my childhood. In pencil and crayons and a child's perspective the drawing shows a man wearing a brown suit sitting in a red chair, a pipe projecting from his mouth. He appears to be smiling and a wiggly line of smoke rises from the pipe. On the ledge beside him a turntable arm touches a black disk. A pencil-line leads from that turntable to a large wood-paneled console radio with a clock-like dial. Three heavily-penciled musical notes hang in mid-air by the radio. There he is, my father in his chair next to the record player, to the left of of the fireplace. And there is my brother Phil's signature.

Those musical notes from Daddy's records no doubt inspired my brother to learn the trombone. I recall the evening Phil and some of his high school band friends brought their instruments and took over our living room. My father got out his saxophone and joined the boys' band, trumpets, trombones and all, filling the house with informal renditions of tunes by Sousa and Gershwin. My father was delighted, and proud of his son.

In high school Phil stood out, a hotshot. He played football and built up his shoulder muscles swimming butterfly on the team that took State two years in a row. He had popular friends, dated popular girls, and starred in the Junior Play. He knew everyone. I entered high school in his senior year. To his chagrin cute girls started to come up to him, and say, "Oh, are you Nancy Clark's brother?" Worse, in his last term in school, I was the only girl in his Algebra III class, and I got the A.

During his last Christmas holidays at home, when he was almost eighteen, Mother downed several drinks to get up her courage to tell Phil she was pregnant. My brother, his hair slicked back, shoes shined, was heading out for a date. Mother realized she would be changing into maternity smocks soon, so, bolstered by the bourbon glow, cornered Phil in the front hallway. She looked him in the eye, "I'm...you're getting another sister or a brother..." I had a glimpse of his face. "In July." He blushed, broke free of her arms, opened the door, and disappeared. Later he claimed not to be embarrassed, that he was old enough to realize that his parents might still be "doing it."

ॐ

In 1953, at the ceremony we witnessed, Phil graduated with an engineering degree and a commission as an ensign in the United States Navy. He would be able to pay the tuition for my last two years of college, a tradition that we continued down the line, sister helping younger sister as best we could.

ॐ

1953

Preparing to go back to college after the trip to New York, I pulled away and rejected my father. I can't recall any concrete images of him from that troubled fall and can only assume he settled into his chair, into his music. I focused on getting my clothes ready for the fall and spent hours in the "nursery" off the kitchen whipping up several tailored dresses on my mother's ancient sewing machine.

Some of my disdain for "my poor sick father" came from the realization that he was working class. While Grandfather Clark, as a newspaper publisher, had been "somebody," and Uncle Jack managed the business and engaged in civic life—they both wore suits to work—my father was a printer. He seldom wore a white shirt, tie, and jacket, and when he did he could hardly wait to shed them. I liked the photos in the scrapbook of his 1929 adventure because I could see he was driving around California and Arizona in his flashy sport Chrysler wearing a three-piece suit. He hoped he'd be taken for a college man. My class detector was being honed at Stanford. My dorm friends didn't need to know that my father went to work in serge pants and a blue chambray work shirt. That he got his hands dirty. But I knew it.

༈

Was he really *non compos mentis?* I'd heard this phrase bandied about years earlier but never expected to apply it to my father. Looking back at myself, I see a twenty-year-old college student forming and consolidating her sense of identity, only beginning to understand her strengths. She had vague hopes of doing something in the world. She felt proud to be among bright, interesting and exciting students. How could a girl with promise have a father whose sanity is in question?

His troubles marred my self-image as an aspiring, educated, upwardly-mobile person.

His troubles kept me from wanting to have an adult father-daughter relationship.

They diverted me from acknowledging my own self-protecting pride.

If Mother didn't want to be a woman with a sick husband, I surely didn't want to be a girl with an unpresentable father.

Kearny, 1949 at Cohassett Beach

cA Silver cAnniversary

Kathy, like Kristy and Nancy before her, is very much Daddy's girl.
— Dorothy Clark

Clearing Mother's things out of her last rented storage locker, in Sunnyvale, California, we came across five milk crates full of naked, black 78 rpm shellac records. Though far from a unique treasure, we decided to stash them in my sister Kristine's nearby garage. And forgot about them. One day, on a visit some time after Mother died, we were poking around in that garage.

"How would you like to listen to one of your father's records?" my brother-in-law asks. He is hauling the milk crates out from under piles of books and sweeping away the cobwebs.

"With pleasure," say I. He sets a record player on the lawn beside the driveway and I dust off a brittle shellac record, easily seventy years old. The label lists Louis Armstrong and Benny Goodman. Outdoors, the sound seems small and scratchy, but as the young Satchmo swings into "The Blues" I am transported from the quilt on Kristine's lawn to the rug in front of the fireplace, near my father's chair. That red chair with the knobby feet in Phil's drawing. I don't recognize the melody, but the rhythm, the phrasing, the timbre of the trumpet, the mellow trombones, all bring me home, to the warmth of the fire, the cedar beams, my father's concentration as he resonates with every phrase.

౷

My father, again in his chair in the corner, selects a record from a hutch. He sets it on the single-play turntable and lowers the needle into the starting groove without setting down his drink. He stokes up his pipe and absorbs Dorsey's pure melodic line in "Song of India," then Benny Goodman's embellishments on "The Wang Wang Blues." Record after record, puff after puff of smoke, ice cubes clinking in his glass. In a while, with Glenn Miller spinning, he feels the conductor's cue, sets down the pipe and glass and puts his imaginary trombone to his lips. He moves the unseen slide with his right hand, in and out, perfectly matching the melody, even to the quaking vibrato on the high notes.

One of his favorite records was "My Heart Belongs to Daddy." Yes, I'd think, while it played. It seemed true to me, but I knew nothing of Sugar Daddies then. He had courted Mother years earlier with the great music of the 20s and 30s—Ted Lewis, Jack Teagarden, Armstrong. He played it all for us. Clearly my brother loved it. How could we not be Daddy's girls?

My father favored and admired his son, and I was jealous. I'd wanted his approval and more, his respect. Mother would say I was "the apple of Daddy's eye," but didn't she really mean just that he doted on his daughters? Certainly *she* did. Years later my husband was shocked at how easily she'd boast about one of us or a grandchild in a manner his family considered gauche.

Still, the fact that I've been writing about my father, his life and his trade, for so many years tells me something about what Mother meant by referring to me as a Daddy's girl. Even before his illness I was his unconscious resonator. His grief, his trauma, his feelings of rejection, his guilt at being the brother who survived, whatever caused his sadness, seeped into my psyche without my being aware of it. I carried his pain and expressed it in sleeplessness, anxious dreams, nightly grinding of my teeth, a left thumbnail so deformed from thumbsucking that I hid it from everyone. Mother seemed able to shed much of the heaviness. Under a tin roof in life's downpour, she heard the pounding rain but let it run off. It was I who stood below the downspout, drenched.

❧

My father had a sturdy build, long-waisted and short-legged, something of a "chimp," Kristine remembered. As was the case for his son, the bones that are usually longest, the humerus in the upper arm and the femur in the thigh, were short relative to the rest, a challenge for my mother and our dapper clothier neighbor. Shirts were always too big, work pants too long. His forehead grew larger with the years as his brown hair receded. Wide-set eyes peered out from behind huge circular lenses of reading glasses, giving him an owlish look. He was diffident and bashful, until he caught you looking at him while someone else held the floor, provoking him to wiggle his ears. Or he might break into a sheepish grin as if to say, "Don't tell anyone, but I'm feeling pretty good, today." Here was a man who outlived his more favored brothers, who took literally his father's directive that a man get a trade.

He was willing to do the dirty work and to take the back seat. A man not suited to meeting the public—so said the family myth.

My father. No matter that when the stress was too much, guilt clutched his heart and he shut down, pulled back. One thinks here of a butter clam, firmly closed, able to withstand exposure to the sun, holding tight until it feels the cool waters of an incoming tide. Or until forced open in the steaming pot.

❦

Even before his breakdown, my father neglected himself. He hated to take a bath or go to the dentist; he'd spend weeks doctoring a decaying tooth with cotton soaked in tooth pain medicine rather than go sit in Dr. Parpala's chair. He seldom ate breakfast unless there was leftover pie; apple was his favorite. He didn't go to church with us. He didn't belong to the Elks or the Kiwanis or any of the Masonic Orders his father had favored. He held his tongue when we visited friends.

Sometimes friends drop in to visit him. I come awake and hear Bill O'Connor shrieking, "God dammit to hell, Kearny, you can't believe that!" I sneak into the dining room. Bill is perched on the kitchen stool with a glass at his elbow, haranguing loudly while my father is cornered at the tiny kitchen table—they always locate themselves near the ice and water, and can easily down a fifth in a sitting. I try to plug my ears because the voices sound so loud and hateful. Why doesn't Mother get them to be quiet? We all know Bill is a lush, "a no-good Irish drunk," according to his wife. Why can't Daddy push him out the door and go to bed?

❦

After our trip to New York, my father spent hours and days in and out of Pinel's hospital, talking to psychiatrists. I heard later that he was not a willing patient. Maybe he didn't want to talk about the voices in his head. And there were visions, hallucinations, or worse. He was used to being private—don't wash your dirty linen in public, he'd been told. I think of that clam. Any progress from the doctoring would come slowly.

But Mother would always be there, cheering him on. Her talent as a parent was to behave as if everything was going well. Like a good poker player, she kept her cards close to the chest. No one would suspect that she had a bust hand. In Tonawanda I had seen her and Aunt Louise, a former nurse, walk away from the group, deep in conversation. I wondered how Louise could help Mother, beyond commiseration. A year later when we visited briefly in Vancouver, Washington, I saw Mother in a close conversation with her sister Peggy, talk that stopped when I approached, "What did the Doctor say…" drifting away. I didn't pry and she didn't confide any of her problems or concerns to me until years later.

ॐ

1955

The next winter my father was laid low in bed at home for three months with pneumonia and pleurisy, and spent some time at Swedish Hospital in Seattle. The doctors ordered innumerable tests, fluoroscopes and X-rays. But by the spring of my senior year of college he was given a clean bill of physical health. Mother reported on the situation in a letter to her sister Barbara: "So we all breathed a sigh of relief and now wait for some nice weather and time to get him feeling good again."

I came home for my last college spring break wearing an engagement ring. My mother, still writing to Barbara: "Seeing as the 29th of March was our 25th wedding anniversary, we threw a great big party and announced Nancy's Engagement." My missing fiancé was a Fulbright scholar in Germany.

Don't all families go through the motions of normality, spreading out the silver and the china, inviting friends to celebrate a milestone, even when they don't know whether they can look optimistically to another twenty-five years? They want to honor the day, even when they don't know whether they can pay the grocery bill. Why worry that the head of the household might not be able to go back to work? My parents would have a celebration.

The happy couple pose for the traditional cutting of a three-tiered cake, the wedding cake they didn't have when they eloped. Their hands clasp together on the knife's handle. The husband in a dark suit, his hair slicked back, gives a big grin to someone in room, while the wife in a soft matronly polka-dotted dress looks right into the lens of the future.

Noel and Klancy, August 23, 1955

The Two Men in My Life

We have all lost touch with life, we all limp, each to a greater or lesser degree.
— Fyodor Dostoyevsky, *Notes from Underground*

In a calm, flowing script on blue stationery, she wrote: *Kearny, my darling: When you wear this lovely soft shirt, pretend it is my arms around you. I love you very much and pray for your recovery and quick return to home. With love, Pete.* On October 3, 1953 my mother tucked the note in a gift-boxed shirt in his suitcase and drove my father the hundred miles to the Pinel Foundation in Seattle. Years later the note turned up among papers in the suede wallet that had been my father's, recovered, along with his other "personal effects," from the mortuary after he died.

What the doctors at Pinel thought about his nervous breakdown became a closely guarded secret. Mother always knew when her friend Fran O'Connor's husband Bill or one of his brothers had once again gone to a facility for alcoholics in Seattle. But she never admitted to Fran where she had taken Kearny. One could joke about a drying-out tank, but not about a mental hospital. Even if it was a private one. Nor admit that your husband was hearing voices.

News of mental illness would not be shared with the neighbors, nor with me. My father spent some weeks in Pinel, off and on during the years I finished college, married, and started a family. Mother told me almost nothing about his experience there. The hospital closed a few years later, and Dr. Shaw, the psychiatrist who treated him, retired, and later died. I've been unable to locate any of Dr. Shaw's records.

❦

I can imagine how heartsick and worried Mother must have been as she wrote that tender note. I find it harder to imagine what kind of conversations my father would have had with the doctors. Did Dr. Shaw get him to talk about his childhood? Or to identify his voices? He surely asked about his parents.

My father had reasons to think he was not the favored son. His brothers were helped to go to college but he was encouraged to become a printer. He seemed gentle and peace-loving, but my mother later said she thought he covered up strain, resentment, or even anger.

Though he might have liked a chance at college, he did love his craft. Each day in the print shop he fired up the melting pots on the Ludlow, the machine that cast lines for headlines, and the Linotype, so they would be ready for the work of the day—forcing molten metal into rows of hollow-faced matrices to create slugs of type. He combined the slugs into blocks of text, then the blocks into forms for the presses in order to produce finished printed matter. His output went to the offices of the prosperous businesses of the town, his newspaper to subscribers' mailboxes each Saturday.

My father's trade may have poisoned him. Some think that the decline of the Roman Empire was caused by lead leaching out of the pewter cooking pots of the wealthy class into their sweet sauces, causing health problems including sterility. The ruling class did not reproduce, goes the theory, hence couldn't hold on to power. My father was exposed to lead every day; he couldn't avoid getting lead dust on his hands while trimming lead castings. Lead occasionally spurted out of the Linotype, fat droplets like shiny mercury that quickly hardened, and got into the sweepings on the shop floor. Vapors from the molten lead possibly escaped from the hot reservoirs in the two machines. If he failed to wash his hands before eating, he surely ingested some lead.

I wonder now if lead could have been detected in his blood or whether lead exposure might have caused his high blood pressure. Could it have caused his moodiness and the seizures we had not yet heard about, or his "nervous breakdown" at age forty-four, or the failure of his business? And his suicidal thoughts in later years?

Would the possibility of lead poisoning change my view of my father? Would it solve anything to think that his work environment had caused his problems? I might have less fear for my own mental health if I knew his condition were not heritable.

No amount of poison in his blood could change the facts of his situation—he had suffered a mental breakdown and was unable to work. And we weren't talking about it.

༰

Mother waited until I went back to college before she took my father to Pinel. As I said goodbye and boarded the southbound train in Centralia, I was filled only with happy anticipation. I'd had my summer, the job at the shop, then the strange trip to New York. I must have stopped thinking about my father. It's hard for me to recapture what I felt about the man who had become so helpless, so childlike. I know it confirmed my sense that I should find a mate who was not like him, who would not embarrass me. But I expected to finish college and have something to show for it. I had bought into the post-war notion that a woman's place is in the home, but if I chose to work it should be in a woman's field. Elementary Education appealed; as a teacher I would surely be helping society.

ॐ

I may always have wished to date an Eagle Scout. One night in my sophomore year, when a friend's boyfriend included dateless-me in an evening out with the two of them—and then afterward he walked me to the door—I thought that boyfriend was the kind of man I'd like to meet.

I met *him*, Noel, the fall quarter after the fateful drive to New York, at Stanford's Roman Catholic Newman Club. A dorm-mate, Bev, arranged a double-date with fellow hashers, Noel and Don. The three of them worked in the dining hall of the other freshman women's dormitory; I worked at the smaller, Branner, on what was then the "men's side" of the campus. Bev hoped to catch Noel and assigned me to be Don's date. A few weeks later Noel found out that I'd declined Don's invitation to a Big Game party (fancy dress affairs after the Stanford-Cal football game). One didn't turn down Big Game dates. It must have intrigued him. The night after that party Noel called to invite me to the Sunday night "flicks."

Even a mediocre student of French could admire his name. *de Nevers*, Noel de Nevers. The most beautiful name I'd ever heard. There must be a duke in his background. And I'd heard that he had a reputation for being hard to get: no girl ever got a second date. Naïve and impressed, I hadn't thought about how many ways one could interpret that bit of gossip. For example, I learned, he'd taken a date to the Military Ball in San Francisco the year before, she in a proper formal, he wearing his Boy Scout regalia, merit badge sash, and short pants. Lacking a sense of humor, the ROTC Colonel threw them out.

A senior, president of everything he joined, a serious student in Chemical Engineering, and he wrote for the *Chapparal*, the school's humor magazine. He invited me onto the handlebars of his bike for rides around campus. We went to the City (San Francisco) in his '39 Pontiac. He kept a mechanic's coverall in the trunk and could step into it and change a tire in a matter of minutes.

Also in the car he kept an elegant gift box holding two champagne glasses. I didn't wonder who before me might have spent time with him watching bubbles rise in the hollow-stems in a quiet corner of the campus—the stock farm had not yet given way to the Stanford Shopping Center. One night he invited one of my good and dateless friends to go out with us for a movie and a sip. And he walked her to her door.

Here was a cheerful, thoughtful, brilliant, energetic, man, nice to his widowed mother, never surly or melancholy. He knew how to bake biscuits over an open campfire, he was healthy, loyal, trustworthy, clean and reverent. In sum, not a bit like my sick father. I'd found my man.

☙

My parents got to meet him before we were married. It was late August 1954, the summer before my senior year of college, and as it turned out, my last summer at home. I'd spent hours sewing bridesmaid gowns for the weddings of my two best friends from high school. Noel de Nevers of San Francisco hitchhiked through Aberdeen on his way to Germany for the Fulbright year but we were not yet engaged. He was my escort for the first event. I can't forget the scene:

My father is enjoying the fine bourbon at my friend Sharyn's wedding. He advises Noel, "You've got to watch out for these fish-eyed Nielsen women." My mother and her many sisters have pale gray-green eyes, a legacy from their Danish father. My father loosens his tie and warms to his topic. "They'll run you out of town if you don't behave." His mind seems to overflow as he tells a story he must have heard from Mother's grandmother, Henrietta, who raised five children with little help from her newspaperman husband, a periodic drunk. She was a member of the Women's Christian Temperance Union, and parsed temperance as abstinence. In the story as my father tells it, Henrietta finally threw her husband out of the house and out of town, and he was last heard from in Alaska where he possibly provided a model for a shady lawyer in one of Rex Beech's adventure stories. I worry that Noel will think badly of my family if my father keeps going on and on.

My father is just a year into his "nervous breakdown" and unusually talkative, his tongue loosened by strong drink and erratic judgement. He continues to describe the scene of my great-grandmother, the wronged wife shouting from the porch, the drunken husband hunkered down behind the hedge begging for mercy, the woman snapping a horsewhip—he loves that part— the husband running away "with his tail between his legs." My father repeats the story several times, each time more embellished, anxious to hold our attention.

A strange way to entertain a prospective son-in-law, I think, since I, too, am one of the "fish-eyed Nielsen women."

☙

When I drove home for spring break my senior year—the visit that included my parents' anniversary party and the announcement of my engagement— my father was horrified with the condition of the '49 Ford I maneuvered into our driveway. Noel had bought it from his mother, who turned it over to me as she headed off to Europe. I planned to drive it back to Palo Alto, then to Ann Arbor, and in August, to New York. My father, more doting than practical, insisted on having a rebuilt engine, new tires, and a first-ever heater installed in the six-year-old sedan. He didn't want his daughter to face a Michigan winter unprepared. Noel thought none of this was necessary—and would have said so in no uncertain terms, had he been there—but managed to write my parents a gracious note thanking them for what he termed their "wedding gift." Though I didn't think about it then, I wonder how long it took my mother to pay the automotive company that did the work, a bill they could ill-afford.

A Wedding

A tiny snapshot from August 1955: a young couple cutting a two-layered wedding cake. The bride's uncle caught the pair, smiling, focusing on the cake-knife. They look so young. It was not a wedding in the bride's home, nor was it an elopement, not exactly.

We *were* young. Freshly graduated, I had driven cross-country to meet Noel, the fiancé I hadn't seen for a year as he debarked from the *Berlin*, (formerly the *Gripsholm*) onto Pier 97 in New York City. We had little time to be alone to get reacquainted in the rush to get blood-tests and obtain a marriage license at the New York City Hall. His mother, sister-in-law and brother had flown in, and we all drove to Buffalo. Aunt Louise in Tona-wanda, whom my parents and I had visited on the way to New York two years before, had made the arrangements for the wedding. My parents sent a telegram of congratulation.

❧

Everything that led up to this day, the proposal, the engagement, the wedding plan, was accomplished by mail while I remained in California working toward graduation and Noel was either studying in Karlsruhe, Germany or conducting *The Grand Tour* of Europe with his mother.

As a correspondent, I was told, I had failings. My letter writing code must have been: Never acknowledge that you received the other person's letter. Never answer questions. Make no decisions.

My letters flew across the seas to a fluent letter-writer, a man accustomed to a weekly exchange by mail with his mother, each commenting on things the other mentioned. Letters hardly profound, yet they communicated.

In a letter to my parents that spring I wrote: "I received an irate letter from my fiancé" for not answering questions about possible wedding dates. Further, still writing, I had to tell him, "I didn't ask the gynecologist about the rhythm method or my cycle." He needed to pin down a schedule that gave time for a wedding and a honeymoon before his graduate classes began in Ann Arbor. The plan required reservations by ship and plane. When I agreed to the schedule that he, in desperation, put forth, I reported to my parents that it felt like I was "capitulating."

Strange truths sometimes flow onto a page when I set my sixty-words-a-minute fingers on a typewriter keyboard. With my fiancé so far away for so long, I felt pulled in two directions that spring. My program in elementary education called for a fifth year. My classmates would go on to get a proper year of student teaching and earn a master's degree, which I would miss. In spite of how demanding and rational his letters seemed—to encourage me to learn the language he only wrote his endearments in German—I certainly didn't want to lose him.

So, that passive-aggressive response rings true. *Capitulating.* That's one letter my mother could have thrown out.

❧

The church of St. John the Baptist was needlessly large. Noel's smartly dressed mother sat in the front row, his brother and sister-in-law stood with us as witnesses. They didn't stand long, this was not a Mass, just a Catholic wedding ceremony. We'd dressed simply, I in a white linen sheath, he in a dark suit. Aunt Louise, her husband, their children, and two of their friends, sat on the bride's side. The rest of the pews in this austere New-England-colonial-style church remained empty.

There must have been music because my new husband had to pay an organist. I'd cashed my last savings bond to get to New York, and claimed not to have heard any music. I was grateful that he took care of it, and also the bill for the flowers, and the cake. These were things my aunt could not afford, things my parents, so far away, were not aware of.

Perhaps, if I had written to them . . .

ॐ

There was no champagne to go with the wedding cake we cut in Aunt Louise's modest Tonawanda living room. Uncle George, a struggling neurophysiology researcher with four children, served lab alcohol in juice glasses as if it were the most normal and gracious thing to do. The morning of the wedding I'd helped the young cousins tuck in shirttails and button up their Sunday-best so we could get to the church, and, given my empty wallet, never thought about what my uncle might offer the guests. My father would at least have served highballs of blended bourbon and water. Noel's mother was shocked, and I sensed that I, and my family, would be judged harshly for this gaffe.

Noel's brother Vince and his wife decorated the green Ford with the usual clutter, and painted phrases in white on all sides: "Just Married," and "Niagara Falls today, Hot Springs tonight." Noel excused Jackie's use of red nail polish on the windshield as justifiable retribution for his role in decorating and disabling the get-away car at their more elaborate wedding three years earlier. On the way out of town we stopped at a drugstore for polish remover and a basal metabolism thermometer with instructions on how to practice the rhythm method, the ostensible Catholic form of "birth control."

Niagara Falls' walkways and viewing platforms were mobbed by adolescents in Boy Scout uniforms. My Eagle Scout husband felt right at home, but I was self-conscious: They must have known we were newlyweds, that we'd slept through the motel's checkout time, and I blushed at the thought.

On the shores of the many Finger Lakes he taught me to skip rocks. We talked, and walked, and drove in a four-state loop back to Ann Arbor, visiting the Corning Glassblowers, a Pennsylvania Dutch village, and undistinguished auto courts along the way.

Dear family,

Another box from the archive: a thin Capezio shoe box stuffed with letters I wrote to my parents from what they called the "Love-birds' Nest," an awkward upstairs apartment without a separate door near the football stadium in Ann Arbor. Several years' worth of letters: small business envelopes with handwritten par avion, or red- and blue-edged airmail envelopes, cancellations on six-cent airmail stamps, letters typed on newsprint. Most were opened neatly at the flap, but a few had been cut or ripped open at the return address end, indicating that my father had been first to read the mail. I was by then writing in first person plural, and occasionally, still, in third person. Again, I scarcely remember being the young bride who composed these letters.

While Noel immersed himself in graduate studies, every day I faced two sessions of first graders who did not know how to read. The second-grade teacher took me in hand, tutoring me on how to teach reading and how to organize a classroom and keep the children occupied. I'm surprised that the letters from that first hectic year of marriage and teaching don't mention the many Mondays I called in sick with a sinus headache, a problem that went away in the spring when another teacher arrived to take one of the sessions.

That fall I described "the proud look on Noel's face now that his wife wears a B-cup bra." Of whom was I thinking when I sat down to write home? In other letters there were reports of the arrival of painful menses, indicating that I wasn't pregnant, not yet. What must my father have thought about such intimate details? I must really have rejected him as being too sick to be aware of my life.

🍂

When next I visited my hometown and the house I grew up in and the family who lovingly saved these letters, I brought along my husband and our first child, a son. Mother declared the infant the spitting image of my father at the same age and to prove it dragged out of the attic the large framed photo of my father that had hung in J.W. Clark's office, the toddler in the knitted snow suit holding a tin horn. My father was thrilled with this first grandchild, whom we named Clark.

☙

Years later I dared to ask Mother what diagnosis the psychiatrists had given my father in the 1950s, and she let drop, with disgust and incredulity in her voice, the word, "schizophrenia." Clearly she never believed it. But she offered no other explanation for his mental state.

Her archive is silent about this time in my father's life. All those boxes, some of them ignored for years at a time in a storage unit, were clearly set aside in case someone, like me, would want to pore over them. But, tellingly, there was no artifact from the Pinel Foundation stay. No report by Dr. Shaw. I had a dim recollection that my father may have spent time in Steilacoom, a state mental hospital so I wrote to the hospital to see if there was a record of his being there. To my surprise they offered to send me twenty-three pages, replicas of bad carbons of the file describing his tenure there. Though unsure whether I wanted to see them, or whether I would want to share any of the information with my sisters, I proceeded. It took many days to decipher the faded pages of carbon-copied text. A poignant story was my reward.

Washington's Western State Hospital sits beside Puget Sound, just south of Tacoma in Lakewood, on the site of the former Fort Steilacoom, a fertile prairie that once supported a large farm and livestock operation. Verdant lawns, native firs, and flowering ornamentals surround the hospital's many buildings, the whole looking more like a college campus than my idea of a mental institution. The hospital began serving the mentally ill in western Washington in 1871 and is still the largest state-operated psychiatric hospital west of the Mississippi River. I wept knowing that my father needed to go to such a place nine years after my first glimpse of his troubles on that trip to New York. Drawing from what the doctors entered in his hospital files, I imagine the details of his arrival:

It is a clear May evening in 1962, the hour 7:00 pm, and a man looking older than his fifty-three years shuffles in the door of an institutional-looking building on the arm of a well-dressed woman. His clothes hang loosely, as if they belong to a larger man. His left leg drags a bit with every step. The woman guides him to a chair and goes up to the front desk. She asks to meet with an admissions officer.

They are taken down a harshly lit hallway to an interview room. The man sits facing Dr. R.W. Stevens, who will write up an Application for Voluntary Admission. The woman sits in a chair in the corner clutching her purse, dragging on a cigarette. She is his wife and will witness the interview.

The man tells Dr. Stevens that for the last four years he has been seeing visions in the sky and hearing a tape playing in his ears. He says he is much improved because he had a pneumo-encephalogram the day before (a brain X-ray). When asked, he says that he is "on the other side of the tracks where religion is concerned." Dr. Stevens fills in the brief form, which the man and his wife both sign, and the man is admitted to Western State Hospital. The woman leaves. The man is assigned a number and becomes "the patient." He is escorted to an observation room and put on "suicide precaution."

My father, Quentin Kearny Clark became patient number 347330. He was still recovering from surgery for two herniated discs, which left some weakness in his left leg. The hospital doctors soon learned that he had swallowed a bottle of aspirin a week earlier, and that his voices told him: "One bullet would do it."

☙

My father was a broken man in many ways by the time he got to Steilacoom. He felt burdened by a long litany of failures: his illness and a second disastrous fire in the print shop had taken away his livelihood. His body pained him, as did his rotting teeth. He couldn't control the voices in his head, and he felt he had betrayed his family. He hadn't told his wife what the voices were saying, nor why he considered himself impotent—there'd been no sex for the previous four years, she later reported to the social worker. He told the hospital psychiatrist his voices call him a pervert and a heretic.

He told the hospital clinicians a lot of things we children never knew—at that time we ranged in age from thirteen to thirty-one—many of them things we might not want to know, though may have suspected. He admitted he'd had epileptic seizures from about age fourteen until ten or twenty years before, when they stopped spontaneously. He claimed he'd had no severe head injuries in childhood, but he'd had fainting spells recently. Though I wasn't aware of such an interest, he seemed obsessed with religion. The doctors noted that he was cooperative and talked quite normally for a while, so "one almost wonders why he is here until he begins to talk about his weird delusions, hallucinations and visions." He laughed inappropriately at times, they said, and he "is somewhat silly."

❦

Shortly after his admission, someone took a photo of him for the file. I am shocked to see it. Staring out over a black plaque bearing his surname and the date is a stern-faced man with wide, thin lips. He looks like a criminal—they might as well have put that number across his chest. But it *is* my father. He appears to have lost weight, his face thinner than I remember, but still dominated by wide-set eyes and the large forehead, a bit of dark hair. Dark blotches fill the hollows under his eyes. He must have been in a confused state for Mother to have decided to bring him to the hospital. Several times he told the doctors he didn't understand why he was there, because he thought his Tacoma doctor—the surgeon who had performed his back operation—had manipulated his brain to drive away his voices.

Unconvinced, the doctors kept him on suicide precaution for a month before releasing him to an open men's ward.

When he was admitted, Dr. Stevens measured his blood pressure at 160/90, and he weighed 144 lbs. at 5' 6". There is no sign in his records that he was treated for high blood pressure, which a patient with that reading would definitely receive today. He described the voices he was hearing as those of "friends who are both alive and deceased" and he felt these came from heaven. Dr. Stevens described him as anxious.

❦

As I look back on the years of my father's illness, I see my own insensitivity and lack of caring, my lack of curiosity. I didn't hear about his being in Steilacoom until much later. I seldom focused on what was going on at home. I had a husband and, by then, three small children. I had no sense of how hard it was for my sisters, for my parents. I sometimes let my husband's reaction to letters from home (which, alas, I didn't save) become mine—"Not more Perils of Pauline," he'd say, or, when Mother wrote about a cousin's troubles, "Doesn't anything good happen in that town?" and I pulled away. But Mother was in denial, too. She censored what she wrote to me because she couldn't bring herself to admit, even to herself, how bad things were. Her silver-lining detector seldom failed her.

My penance now is to sit in the library scribbling *mea culpas* on a yellow pad, probing memories of scene after scene from those troubled years, from my childhood, trying to understand whether I should have seen the problems, wondering whether a more considerate daughter or more observant older sister might have done something to help. Wondering whether any intervention would have made a difference.

One of my first attempts at writing fiction reveals a lot about my inner struggles. For a creative writing class in the 1990s I chose to write about Ingeborg, a young woman called home from college to help out with the family printing business because of the father's incapacitating, but undisclosed, illness. Mother's Danish ancestors included many Ingeborgs, one of them illustrious as "Big Ingeborg of the Hill." I hoped my Ingeborg would also be strong. To respond to the professor's assignment, the piece was imitative of the first chapter of *The Shipping News*, in which the protagonist Quoyle becomes a newspaper man in a Newfoundland port city. My novel would be called *Shelter Harbor News*.

In order to write the first chapter, I sketched out a whole plot. The young heroine comes back from a fancy college as a terrible snob, learns to run the business, grudgingly discovers there are some worthwhile people in her backwater town, overcomes misunderstandings and scandal, and finally, learns humility and an appreciation for the strengths of her town and herself. A scenario I am relieved I never attempted. A Shelter Harbor I'll never visit.

But on alternate days while entertaining "what ifs," I realize that if the family crisis had occurred at a time when I had fewer responsibilities, I might have gotten drawn into its predicament. While I finished college and started a new life, it had looked from an uninformed distance like things were going to work out for my parents. My mother had been diligent in withholding information, in protecting me. Nine years later when Kris was ready for college, only a miracle could have saved the business. And the shop was gone by the time Kathy's turn came. No faithful daughter Ingeborg ever went home to learn the ropes and carry the family business into the third Clark generation.

☙

What had my father found to talk about with the psychiatrists he met during those difficult years? Surely they asked about his childhood. His early life documented in the assorted albums and framed photos looked innocent and loving enough to me. Did he talk about losses? I resolved to dig deeper into my mother's dusty archive and into the files of the *Grays Harbor Post* to learn more about him, and my grandfather, J.W. Clark, and my father's brothers. I hoped to ferret out my father's hopes and dreams, understand why he ran away, and why he came back. Why had he and my mother eloped, and what happened to cause the downfall of the paper and the loss of the print shop? There are surely more stories, true or rumored or totally irrelevant, buried in the boxes wedged so carefully under my basement stairs.

This elaborate design was executed for an exhibit at the World's Fair in Chicago, 1893. Except for a few lines of type, the printing surface was created entirely by hand by printers who twisted brass rule with pliers to form the figures, the background, and the ornamentation, secured in eighteen pounds of plaster to allow it to be printed. Note that the design is built around a scene from a print shop.

Building the family business: buying the type

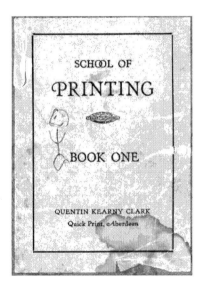

SCHOOL OF

PRINTING

BOOK ONE

QUENTIN KEARNY CLARK
Quick Print, Aberdeen

And here's to Clark! Our genial friend
Who quoteth verses without end.

"And here's to Clark! Our genial friend
Who quoth verses without end."

J.W. Clark, sketched by a South Dakota friend in about 1900.

A Harbor
*M*akes a Home

Grays Harbor will be in at the "Awakening of the Pacific."
— J.W. Clark editorial, 1904

I was born in Aberdeen, Washington, a town with prospects. So were my parents. My father, son of a carpenter-teacher-newspaperman, praised the prosperity signaled by dark, rising plumes from smokestacks of the many lumber mills. My mother, the daughter of a Danish-immigrant druggist, was proud of the number of lumber baron millionaires who'd built their lovely homes above hers, on "The Hill." From her bedroom window as a child she admired the teepee sawdust burners that lined the river, "glowing like huge cats-eyes in the night." The town's workers felt that the wealth of the timber aristocrats should, like the ever-present rain, pour down the hill and into the homes and shops of the working people. During times of unmistakable economic drought those workers threatened a strike.

The story is told that my Clark grandparents came to Aberdeen by mistake. Arriving in Tacoma from South Dakota, J.W. Clark heard of demands for carpenters around Chehalis and Centralia. He and his bride boarded a train apparently bound for Chehalis, but soon found they were headed for Grays Harbor. With his characteristic willingness to take things as they came, he continued to the end of the line.

Aberdeen is the largest city on the coast of Washington. On a clear day snowy peaks of the Olympic Mountains are visible from the area's beaches. The counterweight on the lift bridge across the Wishkah River, still the only way into town from the east, bore an elegant painting of a rocky shoreline and the declaration: "Aberdeen, Gateway to the Olympics." The winning prediction in the annual Rain Derby was usually in the high ninety inches of precipitation, three times that of Seattle. More often than not our town could boast as the home of the National Log-Rolling champion. On this temperate raincoast, the land grew trees: Douglas fir, red cedar, Sitka spruce, western red hemlock, red alder, big leaf maple— enormous trees. As children we learned to read the leaves, the needles, the cones and bark to tell one from another while we learned our ABCs. The City Fathers took credit for all of this and for their cleverness at turning living, breathing cellulose into commercial products.

My grandfather and his sons after him were boosters. They expressed enthusiasm for the town's future in their editorials, in letters and conversations, and in their life decisions,. Aberdeen in its early days looked like a place that could become something. A seaport. A railroad terminus. Lumber capital of the world! A gateway to the Orient! The possibilities seemed endless.

Evergreen forests sheltered virgin timber that had grown undisturbed and to enormous size prior to the arrival of "The Bostons," as the Makah Indians referred to the first white settlers. Grays Harbor's Paul Bunyans, many of whom migrated from the depleted Northwoods of Michigan and Wisconsin, were determined to cut it all.

Booms of logs floated in the rivers, tethered to pilings beside the mills that edged the town sites. Aberdeen burgeoned at the mouth of two rivers as did its Scottish namesake. The Chehalis River, the largest river in Southwest Washington, was navigable by small boats ten miles inland, and scoured out channels permitting the oceangoing vessels of the 1900s to tie up at docks along the Wishkah and the Hoquiam. These rivers carved out a large harbor in their search for the sea.

Tidewater made mudflats, and winter storms often pushed the river onto the land. When my grandparents arrived in Aberdeen, the streets were strips of planking arranged over muddy bogs, edged by wooden sidewalks. Many establishments were built on pilings over the river to avoid the mud and survive during floods.

Ships entered Grays Harbor through the narrow passage between the sandy outcroppings where the river crashed into the swells of the Pacific Ocean. Four-masted schooners and steamships nudged the docks waiting to carry away timber products. Huge mills trimmed logs to ship to Japan, sawmills produced Grays Harbor prime fir for construction, shipyards built sailing schooners from Grays Harbor's own lumber, to ship more of it to foreign ports. Onlookers who'd bought stakes in the vessel under construction wheeled the baby in a pram onto the hillside above the yard to watch the launching and dream of the vessel's seagoing future, anticipating their share in its good fortune. There were chair factories and door factories, and soon, plywood and pulp mills. Brass bands ushered stern-wheeled steamers down greased ways into the muddy Chehalis. In 1918 brass bands paraded with the Army's Spruce Legion Troops who came as wartime strikebreakers to assure the production of quality spruce for airplanes.

Why wouldn't the harvest continue forever? Why wouldn't the harbor with its thriving mills and shipyards, its fishing fleet bringing tons of salmon and tuna to busy canneries, become a hub of importance in Washington? Why wouldn't the railroad recognize Aberdeen's pivotal and ideal location as the northwest portal to the Pacific? Why wouldn't all roads lead to Aberdeen?

My grandfather, J.W. Clark, thought all these things as he settled in this western town.

In the early days Aberdeen was an open city, a haven for loggers who looked for relief from back breaking, dangerous labor in the woods. Streets of bawdy houses, union halls, taverns and flop houses sprang up at this place where logs met blade and boat. The reputation for being a rough town lasted well past my high school years. We believed our town's unsavory reputation explained why sororities at the University of Washington didn't like to pledge girls from Aberdeen. We all knew where the red light district was, and we knew the names of the most infamous (and successful) madams, as did *Look* Magazine, which in 1952 declared Aberdeen one of the "hot spots" in America in the "Battle Against Sin."

Early explorers to this region complained about storms, steady rains and overcast skies, but J.W. took quickly to the climate of "good old Washington." What he especially liked about Aberdeen's weather, he noted in a letter: "the rain washes the air clean and puts color in people's cheeks." The downtown burned down on "Black Friday" in the fall of 1903 but was soon rebuilt in bricks and stone.

ॐ

"An intellect like J.W.'s was hard not to notice," a journalist later observed. J.W. found work in Aberdeen as a carpenter, and joined the union. The Carpenters' Union had acquired a newspaper, and quickly asked J.W. Clark to run it and its working print shop. In the resulting weekly, *Grays Harbor Post,* he exposed graft and collusion to control prices among other papers competing for the legal notices, and won for himself the contract from the

County. The steady income from the obligatory legal advertising ensured the *Post*'s survival into the 1960s. The many offices of the sawmills and logging operations needed to keep records; J.W.'s print shop catered to their printing needs.

ॐ

We shall have a city.

In one of my archival boxes there is an oak nightstick. I'm told it once hung in my grandfather's office, a memento of the winter he and five-hundred other "respectable" businessmen agreed to be vigilantes.

In 1911 the IWW (Industrial Workers of the World), called Wobblies, selected Aberdeen for their latest Free Speech campaign and threatened to shut down the mills if the City Council didn't allow them to tout their radical ideas on its street corners. The IWW planned to organize workers from all industries and trades into one big union, and claimed that "the historic mission of the working class is to do away with capitalism." The city fathers decided to arm themselves with axe handles and "unromantic hickory wagon spokes" to run the Wobblies out of town.

But J.W.'s weapon was nothing like a wagon spoke. It feels good to the hand, a well-turned object with a newel, grip and knurl and a nine-inch bat section, sturdy enough to do real damage to a skull. Tiny indentations on the central axis at each end show that it was spindled on a wood lathe, probably at the local chair factory. In spite of the grime accumulated during years hanging in a print shop, it still smells like a fine piece of wood. He wanted us to remember this story—the nightstick is inscribed in ink: "I.W.W. Nov–Apr 1911-1912." The piece of baling wire carefully twisted around the handle into a hook allows it to hang now on the wall in my office, a testament to my strong-willed grandfather's desire to protect and defend his hometown from those he considered dangerous agitators.

Somehow I can't picture my book-reading, poetry-reciting small-town-editor grandfather as a member of a crazed mob. He was a union man, but didn't see any good in the Wobblies, who "hoboed" into town after town, disrupting normal business and clogging the jails. I wonder if he ever wielded his billy club in anger on one of those nights when Aberdeen's burghers conducted a midnight sweep of the jail and "escorted" all the

Wobblies they could find to the road out of town. I like to think he stood on the sidelines, acting as a reporter rather than a roughhouser.

౿

Once settled in their new town, J.W. and Marie became strong magnets, drawing almost her entire Norwegian family by twos and threes from South Dakota to settle near them in Aberdeen and Hoquiam. In a 1913 photograph my young father sits on a small trike, a Flying Dutchman, surrounded by his brothers, their parents, many uncles, many aunts in full length white dresses, and his Norwegian grandmother.

Having lived so long in Utah's sunbathed desert, I've often wondered why my grandfather would leave the prairie and his family to come to a damp and gloomy place like Western Washington. I mentioned this to a friend.

"If you'd ever been to South Dakota, you wouldn't have to ask." My friend had grown up in Chicago and thought he understood why they left Canistota. Recalling my grandfather's trophy room, I think I understand, too.

Up to the age of fourteen, J.W. lived in central New Jersey, amid established towns, piney woods and breezes from the sea. He may not have taken to the Dakotas' endless prairie where grass stood three feet deep, where buffalo no longer roamed, where wheat, barley and corn were the most exciting things coming up around his town. When he was nineteen, the plains experienced a great blizzard. The January day[1] "broke dark and lowering; a light steady snow was added to the foot that had already fallen. By 10 o'clock the region was blanketed with fog. Suddenly, without warning, the wind changed and the temperature tobogganed [down] nearly 70 degrees. The wind continued to rise and soon a 60-mile gale was howling mercilessly across the open expanses. Steel-like snow in blinding eddies was hurled with withering intensity at whatever object happened to be in its path...When the storm had subsided, it had written a pitiful tale of suffering and death across its icy pages."

J.W. and his parents survived, but some 200 hapless souls perished. This was not a climate for a man who loved the outdoors. Like his father, he

---

[1] Jan 12, 1888. Page 295-96, *South Dakota: A Guide to the State*. Compiled by the Federal Writers' Project of the Works Progress Administration. State of South Dakota, Hastings House, 1938.

was as an avid "wing shooter"—ducks and geese during migrations, and prairie chickens. Perhaps he tracked an occasional deer. He read widely and had already begun to collect books on many subjects. A favorite was *Wild Animals I Have Known* by Ernest Thompson Seton.

Perhaps stories about abundant and wondrous wild animals lured J.W. and his bride to the Pacific Northwest. His sons thought he was following the exhortation of Horace Greeley—"Go West, young man"– though when Greeley spoke out he may have meant the West that lay beyond the Appalachians, perhaps Ohio.

After settling in Aberdeen, J.W. managed to spend a few weeks each year in the Olympic Mountains accompanied by dogs, mules, friends, and a guide. An account of each trip into America's last wilderness made it into the *Post*. The trophies he left behind attest to his love of the hunt: among them a stuffed bobcat with impressive ear tufts and an enormous bearskin rug with a large, heavy head and claws as long as his sons' fingers.

Nothing about Aberdeen or the Olympics would have reminded J.W. of South Dakota, and that was probably what he intended.

ॐ

J.W. took to newspaper publishing with alacrity. On the new masthead he declared that his newspaper would "Stand for the United Interests of Grays Harbor" and explained his philosophy in his first editorial: "The *Post* holds to the economic law that discrimination means economic death and therefore believes in the death of discrimination." The paper would be strictly independent, would encourage citizens to vote intelligently, and would watch out for the public good. "The unskilled man is against it, both for a job and for pay....If you learn a trade it is a sheet anchor in time of storm...I would like every boy in America to learn a trade. A trade is an education in itself and it makes a fellow more or less independent.

"The great volume of the world's necessary work is done by the man in overalls...He is the one great need in the world of progress."

He was a trade unionist and a Republican. These were not incompatible interests in 1904. A South Dakota newspaper reported J.W.'s new situation to its readers: "Editor Clark, of the Aberdeen *Post*...is almost too good a fellow to be spoiled by contamination with newspaper work. As we remember him he was a populist of the populists in politics, but a very nice gentleman taken all in all."

The world he chronicled in the early issues of the *Post* contained hoboes, socialists, democrats and professional beggars. He wrote about cows inside city limits, ships running aground, people still housed in shacks months after the big fire, and a Teamsters Union Grand Ball. Soon he found something meatier: A FRAUD ON THE CITY! A large local mill was found to have an un-metered water line from the city water supply, and an officer of that mill was chairman of the City Council Water Committee. J.W. urged taxpayers to demand a thorough investigation. He ended each exposé with the comment: "Let in the light." Within a month the mill agreed to pay its share of the water tax ($619.11) and the committee chairman resigned. The *Post* headline: "*And the Light Shone In.*"

Over the years, as his sons were growing up, J.W. documented elections, bond issues, suicides, drownings, trials, patriotic parades, and the industrial conflicts in his community. Aberdeen was a lumbering hub. Logs came from the woods, towed down the rivers in floating booms, they came by train, and later they came by truck. The mills piled logs or lumber into three-masted schooners and steam ships; with the extension of a railroad link to the harbor, long snaking trainloads of lumber headed east. The Harbor area boasted some 50 sawmills, one of which was for a time the largest mill in the world. Chimney stacks spewing smoke from pulp mills and sawmills were featured on page one of the *Post* to signify that all was well. As J.W.'s sons grew up and attended schools in Aberdeen, the woods provided great wealth to hardworking loggers and mill owners and to the businesses that served them. The boys' days were partitioned by the screeches and whistles of the mills, their walks to school dampened by rainfall, their nights brightened by the lines of glowing sawdust burners along the river.

Labor troubles inhabited Grays Harbor as naturally as barnacles and mussels cling to pilings, as casually as rainwater puddles in rough roads. Turn your back on a clearing and it filled with alder seedlings. Turn your back on workers and you got a slowdown or a strike or a dispute about which union has the right to represent the men in the mill.

Even as J.W. was willing to oppose the working class Wobblies, he was not afraid to challenge the questionable practices of unscrupulous mill owners. One memorable campaign pitted him against a trap-shooting friend who ran Pope & Talbot's Grays Harbor Commercial Company in

Cosmopolis, a mill the workers called "The Western Penitentiary" because working conditions were so bad. The operation had a turnover rate as high as 600 percent. J.W. illustrated his exposé with photos of the shabby workers' quarters in stark contrast to the luxurious home of the manager. Conditions soon improved.

My father and his brothers would have heard J.W.'s strong opinions growing up. They saw that if J.W. liked you, as he did the Carpenter's Union Secretary and his bride, you would appear on the front page of the *Grays Harbor Post*. If not, you might be vilified in that same space, or you might be told to meet him in the woodshed.

When my father inherited the print shop with all the presses, the typesetting machines, the type, he was reluctant to give up anything because it had been his father's. I am doing the same thing. I'm happy that my father held onto the oak nightstick and so much else that I can examine to try to understand his life.

Grays Harbor would suffer the fate of small towns all over America, but we didn't know that. Weren't we special? That Aberdeen and Grays Harbor and the Northwest raincoast could not and did not live up to its promise is one of the challenges of the region which J.W. had to face in his thirty-two years as editor of the *Post*, a challenge that passed on to his sons.

J.W.'s Boys
From left: Perry Jack, Kearny

Printing Runs in the Family

A.J. Cummings, printer and statesman, said that the newspaper composing room might rightly be considered the poor man's university.
— Lessons in Printing

When in 1908 my grandmother Marie Clark went into her third confinement, she was hoping to give birth to a girl. She planned to name the baby Marie after herself. The doctor handed her another strong, healthy but howling boy, and what could she do? Here was the infant who would become my father. She had no name for him.

She had seen her first two boys model themselves after their father, J.W. They bowed to his voice, they trailed in his shadow, adopted his attitudes, imitated his gestures. She may have studied her husband's face as he dandled one of the boys on his knee and recited his favorite Kipling: "Yours is the Earth and everything that's in it, / And—which is more—you'll be a Man, my son!"

Marie thrived in the company of girls, of women, and there were no such poems for the likes of her. As far back as she could remember she had sisters, and in her first ten years, her mother gave her three more, all of whom she dearly loved. She was pleased when her parents, and then one by one, each of the sisters, left South Dakota to join her in this rugged western community. They too would produce sons. Only the eldest, Christine, gave birth to a girl, Mildred, who would be known as my father's "only girl-cousin."

My grandfather gave the new baby two strong masculine names: Quentin from the title character of one of Sir Walter Scott's *Waverly Novels*, (*Quentin Durward*) and Kearny after General Philip Kearny. It is likely that J.W. admired the General's courage. Though General Kearny lost an arm fighting with Sam Houston in the Mexican War, in the Civil War he rode ahead of his troops with the reins in his teeth and a sword in his remaining hand until he was slain at Second Manassas.

This son, who became my father, always disliked that first name and chose to go by Kearny,

As he grew out of his cradle and into the small carriage, as he toddled and then ran along the planked sidewalks of West Market Street, he was kept in white dresses, ruffled bonnets and sweaters. Though this garb was not unusual for the time, I wonder if my grandmother intended the dresses for the daughter she didn't have?

When his own son, Philip Kearny, came along, my father must surely have been pleased to see him decked out for his third birthday in a boy's cap, jacket, and short pants, looking like he was ready for anything.

❦

As Kearny grew up, he had two brothers ahead of him—Perry, the fleet-footed athlete; Jack, the sweet-talking charmer and practical joker. Brothers to lead the way, to take the flack, to wear down their parents' hopes and aspirations, perhaps monopolize their attention. The youngest was expected to become part of the group—the gang of three told to stand up straight, listen to the grownups, speak only when spoken to.

The brothers led the way. If Perry played softball, so did Kearny. If Jack played the trombone, so did Kearny. The older boys in their turn became editors of the school publications, and so did he. If they worked in the print shop, then so did he. They learned to drive, joined the National Guard, and went to college. He meant to follow in their footsteps.

He hoped for college, but on the way he would teach himself to be a printer.

❦

I couldn't believe my good luck when an old friend, Pat O'Connor, walked into my 1995 book signing in Aberdeen holding a small package, and asked me, "Would you like to have your Dad's *Printing Lessons*?"[2] Pat had been a year ahead of me in school and our parents were close friends. He worked at the shop, and when my father became sick and was unable to work, Pat kept the shop going and eventually bought it.

Would I like the *Printing Lessons*? His sister standing nearby recalled hearing me rave on and on, how hard I'd looked for them, how pleased I was

---

[2] The book was *Cohassett Beach Chronicle: World War II in the Pacific Northwest* by Kathy Hogan, edited by me and Lucy Hart, Oregon State University Press, 1995.

to have them, how wonderful he was to have saved them all these years, how I couldn't believe he carted them around from house to house since he dismantled the old print shop, just hoping someone would want them. He was right, I wanted them.

It's hard to explain why I have such an investment in the bound volumes of my father's correspondence course in printing. There's curiosity, of course. For me they take the place of the college he didn't get, a higher education he accomplished by himself. Completing the lessons required motivation and self-discipline and a commitment to his future, traits I could understand. The union card, when he achieved it, gave him a trade and thus more status in the eyes of his father.

❦

The lessons fit into seven small volumes, each containing 9 or 10 ten-page lessons, and had survived at least two shop fires and several moves of the whole establishment. They had been prepared and published by the Allied Printing Trades Council and approved in the 1920s by the International Typographical Union, which boasted: "Printing offers many opportunities to the man who is considering a profitable and enjoyable trade or profession as his life work."

They teach the art of *Composition*, which is the name for what printers have done since moveable type was introduced five hundred years ago. However in the late nineteenth century, typesetting was revolutionized, first by mechanical typecasting and typesetting machines such as the Ludlow and the Linotype. The lessons start with elementary composition, then move on to composition for display work, job work such as stationery and business forms, design and color, newspaper practice and advertising composition. One long unit covers English for Printers, an extensive exposition of the rules for punctuation, grammar, and spelling, to ensure that the printer learns to recognize and take pride in the proper use of the language.

My father studied the text in each lesson, marking a few things here and there in the margins, and then wrote or typed answers to the Examination Questions at the lesson's end. Those he mailed to the examiner at the Bureau of Education of the ITU in Indianapolis, Indiana, from whom he received a score, encouragement and another lesson. At some point he gathered the lessons of a unit together like the signatures of a book, and bound them in cardboard with cloth tape and a nicely centered printed label: School of Printing, the union 'bug,' Book One (etc), Quentin Kearny Clark, Quick Print, Aberdeen. The label was set in a special Roman font — the intersecting "o"s in "School" is a rarely-seen ligature.

Could this five-pound handful of yellowed, musty pages possibly bring back the quiet man who seemed so at home among the type cases, the presses, the stacks of half-finished jobs, but so like a fish out of water everywhere else?

☙

Looking at the *Printing Lessons,* two questions come to mind—what kind of higher education did they provide to my father, and how much did they really teach about how to be a printer? The only answer I have is that he bound and saved the volumes, just as I saved many of my college textbooks.

The first book of the *Printing Lessons* begins innocuously enough. **Unit 1 Lesson 1**: MATERIAL USED IN TYPE COMPOSITION. The image of a typeset word in script looks out from the page, and though I can't read it, I understand what I'm seeing. Individual pieces of metal grouped together each bear the raised face of a letter upside down and backward. By holding the image before a mirror and inverting it, I see the word *Rapidity.*[3] This is an example of a kerned font, and the student is exhorted to remember that such type faces must be handled carefully to avoid damage to the delicate parts of any letter that project *sideways* from its body.

The lessons in **Unit 1** describe how a page of type is composed by a compositor, standing before a drawer of type, placing one letter or one em quad or spacer at a time, into his composing stick. He then moves these lines of type from the stick onto a galley. The printer or compositor's job is to fill a chase or holding frame entirely with metal in the inverse image of the desired printed page. Some of the metal will consist of lines of set type, the words spaced and justified. The rest of the metal, called furniture, is required to make line spacing, margins or borders, the white space on the paper, and to enable the printer to lock the separate pieces together inside the frame. After it is corrected, a frame is carried to a press for printing.

Each time I pick up one of the lessons it takes over. Fully absorbing the text, rather than scanning, I devour the concepts, the terminology, and start

---

[3] Kunstler Script font

taking notes. The lessons read like family history, the history of a family blessed—or burdened—with a technology destined to become obsolete.

॰

One late summer day, while my grandfather packed up for a hunting expedition with friends, Marie bundled her boys onto the train for California and arrived a day later by ferry at the foot of Market Street in San Francisco. She planned to take them to the 1915 Panama-Pacific International Exposition that celebrated the opening of the Panama Canal.

Kearny was seven years old and San Francisco made a lasting impression on him. This was his first world fair. The three boys, ranging in age from seven to twelve, posed patiently in front of a fountain with a woman in a sari identified only as an "Indian Princess." Marie in a long fitted dress and a spectacular feathered hat allowed herself to pose for a silhouette artist. She later inscribed the tall black image as a gift to her first, and possibly favorite, son Perry. Young Kearny endured many warm days trailing his mother and brothers through elaborate and majestic avenues bordered by palaces of chicken wire and plaster, and aisles of bronze and plaster sculptures, all declared to be art.

> He had loved "Frisco" ever since, at seven,
> he trailed his mother's skirts through an Exposition.
> As she lectured them on Culture and Art,
> his older brothers whispered and pointed
> at the white plaster nudes.[4]

From their rented rooms at 1000 Union Street on Russian Hill in San Francisco the family's youngest son scrawled a postcard in awkward cursive: "Dear papa I wish you could come to the fair. I saw the tower of Jewels. I saw an aeroplane. Art Smith [The stunt pilot]. I saw a little train. Sousas Band on the grounds. good by. Kearny Clark"

He may have resolved right then to come back to this exciting city on the bay when he grew up.

In Los Angeles, wearing a sailor suit and hat, he perched happily on the outrigger seat of a cart as his brothers held the reins of the cart's "horse," a

---

[4] Excerpt of a poem I wrote, "What do you say to a naked lady?" telling the (possibly true) story of my father running into Sally Rand backstage at the Golden Gate International Exposition in 1939 in San Francisco.

large ostrich. Marie in a broad-brimmed sunhat hovered nearby smiling for the photographer.

Meanwhile J.W. had his 1915 adventure documented in a formal portrait. Marie and her boys appear clean and well-dressed in the photos of their journey. In contrast, the hunters home from the hills project a more casual image. Four men stand at the end of the trail in rumpled hats and rough hiking clothes and tall boots beside a mule still laden with gear and a large carcass, their three hounds panting and tugging on leashes. The photograph is labeled "Back from the Olympics — Sept. 20, 1915." I wonder if it was on this outing that my grandfather bagged the cat whose stuffed and mounted figure we later gave to the high school, home of the Aberdeen Bobcats.

❦

My grandfather intended to see his sons follow in his footsteps. But in which set of shoes? He had been a carpenter, a teacher. He became a sportsman, an editor, a businessman. A man of so many talents, it could not have surprised him to find those talents shuffled and dealt out at random among the three boys.

The firstborn, Perry, never found a sport he didn't excel in, and seemed likely to be the one to join his father on hunting expeditions. He gathered advertising for the two high school publications. He could do that for the *Post*. The second, Jack, was outgoing and more interested in leading and entertaining people, whether by improvising at the piano or telling stories or being class president. He could be a businessman, a fine print shop manager. Kearny, his youngest was calm, quiet, a careful worker. He could be the back shop man, the printer. J.W. raised his boys to follow the admonitions of Elbert Hubbard, founder of the Roycroft Colony in western New York—respect The Boss's authority.

All would be right in J.W.'s world, Quick Print Co., the printing firm of Clark and sons.

❦

Printing had come a long way from the time of Gutenberg, and even from Ben Franklin's day, when a printed page was composed one letter at a time and printed one hand-fed sheet at a time. As my father was studying the lessons, mechanization was advancing into those print shops and newspaper plants that could make the capital investments. But most printed pages still came from hot type composition and inked lead pressed on paper. The lessons were relevant.

The printer's education in these lessons includes some history of writing and printing, a bit of civics to cultivate an appreciation for a free press, the arithmetic of the printers' yardsticks, points and ems, and lots of artistic training. The lessons argue that many of the jobs are valuable and desirable, and while the composing room is the poor man's university, then "work in a newspaper proofroom is a continuous post-graduate course."

Some inspiring thoughts appear in the pages: "Our trade of printing really started there on clay, long before the people in Baghdad started to erect the tower of Babel" in Babylonia, before 3000 BC. "The compositor and the sign painter are producing and selling words...People who buy words do not want to pay for misspelled or misused words."

Completion of the lessons would allow my father to join an elite group of people focused on words, people who cared deeply about producing a quality product. He would progress to a place where he belonged, where his expertise didn't depend on the expectation of others, where he could feel capable and confident. "A lesson a week makes a printer unique," must have seemed like a fine aspiration.

৳

In the summer of 1922, days before Perry's twentieth birthday, the family gathered in the Essex touring car for a trip to Lake Quinault, less than two hours away. Here's the scene:

The boys and a friend are in good spirits, entertaining their parents with college songs and jokes. Perry has finished a year at the University of Washington, where he played football and joined a fraternity; Jack has just graduated from high school. The boys work up a sweat clearing out a space near the lake for a tent and go for a swim. Upstream of the lake, the Quinault River drains a long, rugged canyon in the Olympic Mountains with headwaters in the Enchanted Valley, one of J.W.'s favorite hiking destinations. The tree-lined lake is deep and always cold.

As they swim toward a distant float, Perry cries out and disappears. Kearny and Jack are unable to locate him in spite of many desperate dives in the dark water. When the alarm is raised, other picnickers come to help; after twenty-two minutes, someone with a trolling line locates the body. A group of Aberdeen Boy Scouts builds a fire on the shore in hopes of warming him back to life. No amount of artificial respiration or heat revives him.

☙

This day is described in painful detail in a news story from the *Grays Harbor Post* that was pasted into one of the family albums. I heard about it as a child many times. I recently interviewed a former scout and long-time friend who helped build that futile fire and recalled the scene.

My father was just fourteen. The drama of Perry's death, as my mother told it, always included a painful fact—his mother no longer recognized him. After reading further in the old scrapbooks and journals, I imagine another scene:

Just home from the lake, his mother goes into her bedroom. It is quiet for a while. Then she rushes to the bathroom to wash her hands. She rubs and splashes feverishly as if she were Lady Macbeth trying to remove King Duncan's blood. Then she goes to bed. And stays there. Young Kearny has never seen his father look so helpless. His mother gets up only to attend the funeral, emotionless, a dark silhouette in a black felt hat. Her first son in the ground, she returns to her bed.

Later they find words and a large ink blot on a page in her journal, the one for that day. The only entry prior to this was the register of births on page one. Two parents, three sons. Otherwise the leather-covered volume that asks only for "A Line a Day" is blank.

In a small, controlled hand, she had written:

morning of July 2, 1922.
   Papa - mama - Perry - Jack - Kearny-
   Jim Palmer - left for Lake Quinault-
   Shortly after 11 o'clock all boys went in for
   a swim - Perry was drowned - a few minutes later.

His mother is inconsolable. When Kearny is allowed to go in to see her, she calls him Perry.

☙

Printing Lessons **Unit 2** describes leads and slugs, and type metal that is made of lead mixed with antimony, tin and copper. A sketch of a type case and boxes of graduated furniture, the special metal shapes used to fill in blank areas around a line of type, are familiar. I am transported to my father's back shop.

I see myself, probably fifteen years old, enter the passage between type cases and the Linotype machine and stop in the type-setting corner. The tall windows facing G Street are opened a foot or so; they are spattered with dirt, looking like they've never been washed. Below, across the street are the meat market, the Greek's grocery store and the Bright Spot Tavern. Spatters of shiny lead have settled on the black, oiled floor under the Ludlow typecasting machine. The air tastes of tobacco smoke, metal and machine oil. Tall cabinets with drawers full of type fonts dominate the area. A large frame lies on one of the stones, where my uncle Alec is filling in what will be a page of the *Grays Harbor Post*. A lighted cigarette hangs from his mouth. Alec Dunsire is a tall, cock-sure Scotsman with snapping eyes, a gift of gab, and a love of fishing. He is married to one of my mother's sisters, Joan, a timid woman skilled in domestic arts. She is a master seamstress and she is in awe of Alec. He teases—he likes to get a rise out of people, and often there's an edge to the exchange. Near the end of the war he served in San Diego as a marine reserve drill instructor, a perfect fit.

He builds the page of newspaper from blocks of type matter under headlines from the top of the page and blocks of advertisements and boilerplate from the bottom. From his position all the type is upside down and backward. I have been proofreading galleys of text for the week's paper and bring him marked copy. He'll get the corrections from the linotypist and put in the corrected lines. To finish the page, he'll insert small blocks of filler: lame jokes, or small cuts of commercially provided filler, much like today's clip art. When he has a full page he taps it all over with a wooden block and mallet to level the type, then locks it in, turning a special key in the quoins. I haven't thought of that word for years—*quoins* —but I can see the wedge-shaped objects spaced evenly inside the frame holding the type. By twisting the key between its two geared wedges, the quoin expands to secure the page. The finished frame will join others on the huge flat-bed press that prints sheets of four newspaper-size pages at a time. When the paper-bearing cylinder rotates and the huge chase moves back and forth under it, the floor throbs and the whole building vibrates as if a train were passing through.

ॐ

After Perry's death, my distraught grandmother likely suffered a nervous collapse. My chance a few years ago to find out whether she spent time in a mental hospital, as my father's old friend Joel Wolff seemed to be telling me, was lost when his wife interrupted, "Oh, dear, we don't have to talk about those old, sad days." Joel had known my father all his life but in later interviews I was unable to bring him back to this subject.

When Marie died the local *Daily World* reported in the obituary that she "never fully recovered from the loss of her son Perry....[it] was a greater blow to her than even her intimate friends imagined."

My grandfather shared his personal life, the good and the bad, with his readers. In the week's editorial he wrote "through the blinding mist of tears" to thank those many people who had "lightened the tragedy....Perry had nineteen years of useful, happy life....His loyalty to his parents, his brothers, to his schoolmates and to his own town and state was an outstanding characteristic of this Aberdeen boy."

ॐ

My father never went back to Lake Quinault. Its expanse of cold water loomed as a menacing place in the family narrative. I once scribbled a bit of fiction about a married couple who are staying in a cottage at the edge of a beautiful, tree-lined lake. The morning after a large party they ignore the clutter of dirty glasses and ashtrays to go out on the lake in a canoe. A sudden wind comes up, throwing up white-caps and pushing them away from the shore. The woman screams that they must get back, she doesn't want to die leaving behind such a mess, what will people think of her? The man feels powerless as he paddles against the wind and hallucinates about diving time after time into the dark water. I've never been able to finish the story.

The high school my father entered that fall instituted an athletic award in Perry's name, and it was still being offered when we children graduated. There would be no forgetting.

ॐ

Lesson **Unit 9** states that filled galleys should be placed on a clean stone to pull a galley proof. The concept of a clean stone is absurd. This is a print shop. Its product is black on white, and printing ink is a mixture of carbon black or soot and a binding agent. The stone is a huge slab of once-smooth marble built into a waist-high wooden table. Printers stand around every side to work. Ink-covered brayers rest on ink-dabbed copper plates near each work area ready to roll ink onto type. Inky rags and kerosene cans are handy next to the frame of type, ink finds its way into the very grain of the wooden frame of the stone, into the pores of the marble, into the pores of the printers' hands. Ink stains rarely succumb to the rough grains of Lava soap handy at every grimy wash basin. The only time anyone would even attempt to clean the stone is before the occasional party.

It's a Friday afternoon and I'm at the shop after school, after the paper has gone to the post office. The presses are silent. Liquor bottles and a bowl of ice stand on one of the cleared stones. My father and some other men, including the pressman, lean around the other. Each gets a turn with the cup, shaking it and rolling out the dice near a patch of green bills. Someone says, "Come on, snake eyes!" Uncle Alec is running the show. I want someone to explain the game to me, but I can't ask. My father, the sleeves of his chambray work shirt rolled up, a glass of bourbon at his elbow, looks happy as he gets his turn. I can't tell who is winning.

❧

The fall of 1922 found Kearny Clark the only son at home. Perry was in a grave in Fern Hill Cemetery, Jack had gone off to college at Stanford. His mother struggled with grief, and his father was keeping a straight back and a stiff upper lip. Years later my father told the psychiatrists in the mental hospital that seizures (plural) started in his teens and he suffered his first seizure not too long after Perry's death.

He threw himself into schoolwork, and into books. A snapshot captures him lounging with a book in the "reading nook," a corner nestled behind a tall wood-burning stove in the dining room. He may have read all of the Bret Harte, Washington Irving, and H. Rider Haggard books that lined shelves in his father's library. He learned to play the full range of saxophones and the trombone. He enjoyed music and joined every musical group in the high school including the men's chorus. His band, the Blue and Gold Melody Men, performed for assemblies, the school variety show,

Hi Jinx, and school dances. He was younger than his classmates because of two promotions in grade, so he may have been happier making the music rather than having to ask a girl to dance. Where Jack had been elected president of everything, Kearny was more likely to be vice president, often as the sidekick to a buddy, such as lifelong friend Bill O'Connor. He worked on the *Quinault* yearbook and, his senior year, served as its editor. The society pages of the *Grays Harbor Post* noted a "crowded social calendar in high school circles" in the week of his graduation, June 1925. Among the many parties mentioned were three at the Clark home, including an "informal dancing party" for my father and eleven friends.

In his graduation class of 136, and the whole school of 420, he was the only student to earn honors in six subjects.[5] The epigraph beside his yearbook photo reads, "A superior man, modest in his speeches, but superior in his actions."

༝

Hand-stitched into a large scrapbook resting in a box in my back closet are ten issues of the *Ocean Breeze* from my own senior year in that same high school. My name is on the masthead, my chatty column appears on page one of each issue. I am embarrassed by some of the headlines and captions that I wrote. One I regret was "Beauty and the Beast" which appeared above the photo of my good friend Ann and a rugged-looking football player named John. As editor I gained another status, I was a bone fide customer of my father's print shop, which had always printed the school's paper. To help the editor, Uncle Alec had created a sample page of headline fonts in several sizes and column widths. Just before going to press, the sports editor and I collected and measured the stories from our reporters, laid out the pages, chose the fonts and wrote the headlines, counting letters to be sure they would fit. As he and I sat at our family's dining table working on the project, my father would walk through, pause, and smile. I could tell he was pleased that I was the editor.

I feel important as I bring the layout to the shop the next day. While the stories are being set on the Linotype, Alec opens font drawers, sets the

---

[5] His friend Karl Bendetsen excelled in only four subjects, as did the girl who gave the valedictory address for Class Night. Bendetsen was the Colonel and main focus of my 2004 book, *The Colonel and the Pacifist: Karl Bendetsen, Perry Saito, and the Incarceration of Japanese Americans during World War II.*

headlines, and casts them on the Ludlow, then follows my plan to make up the paper. He teases me if a headline doesn't fit, and makes me redo it. I am seeing the print shop from both sides, and even though I am the customer, I don't have to pay the bill. I hope my father thinks I'm doing a good job.

ৡ

The week his youngest son was graduating from high school, my grandfather's editorial lauded the Board of Education, the fine teachers, and his adopted town: "Aberdeen has gained a place in the sun as one of the great industrial manufacturing centers of an essential industry" he wrote.[6] He offered words by Nathaniel Hawthorne to inspire the graduates: "Let us each make the best of our natural ability...and with the blessing of Providence we shall arrive at some good end. As for fame, it matters little whether we acquire it or not."

He mentioned that past graduates of the high school had "given a good account of themselves" in various colleges of the Pacific Coast, and that the class of 1925 could boast a high percentage of honor students. He didn't mention that his youngest son was graduating with distinction. He didn't mention that he would not be sending his brilliant "*Benjamin*" to college.

ৡ

A young man peers out of a ship's huge air intake funnel. His smiling face is framed by the shiny bell that looks like an over-sized tuba—young Kearny is taking the place of the horn's mute. I often puzzled over this tiny snapshot in my father's photo album. How did he climb into the tube? At the age at which his brothers, and later, his children, went away to college, my father shipped out.

College wasn't in his future. There was money only for his brother Jack's education. The six-bedroom house J.W. built on West Sixth Street, the big house I remember, may have seemed too large and empty and haunted by his mother's sadness.

While his friends were getting ready to go to Stanford or to the state universities, he packed up his trombone and some clothes and hitched a ride to Portland. It was the summer of 1925 and he had just turned seventeen.

---

[6] Aberdeen's lumber production reached its peak in 1924. The *Post* that year acknowledged the big celebration when the year's billionth board foot was on the dock to be shipped, a level of annual production never again achieved.

He signed on with the *Sunugentco*, a 3,000 ton steam freighter out of New Jersey. In photos it was unimposing, having modest hoists and very little superstructure; most of the cargo (lumber, wheat, sugar, manufactured goods) rode in the holds. He worked two "cruises" as a cabin boy on that ship, and years later told his wife that those sailings were the high point of his life.

The family narrative is that he was too young to go to college. Many young men on the harbor worked on ships as a way to earn some money, and going to sea was thought to be romantic. Stories about the great sea captains of the era when four-masted schooners tied up at Aberdeen's docks often appeared as filler in the back pages of the *Post*.

He did write about college in letters to his Gal Sal a few years later. How might his life have been different if he had spent a year or two listening to professors talk about the wealth of nations or the causes of the Great War? Perhaps he would have developed an interest in science or quantum physics, fields exploding with new discoveries every year of the 1920s. Or would he have found the classrooms stuffy?

His scrapbook includes photos from those two cruises and he is smiling in all of them, looking young and carefree. "[It's] my favorite snapshot, taken in an outside passageway," he wrote later. "The coat and hat are the steward's. That is, I was in the steward's department and while serving the meals, I wore the white coat. The hat was a loan for the picture. The rest of my attire was just as dirty as it looked. In fact very little of the sweat, dirt, paint, and general run of ship's dirt seems to create the atmosphere that I no doubt smelled."

He told another story about "a guy he met" on one of the tours: "he and I have been holding a sort of disinterested correspondence. While we were together on the ship we got to be pretty close friends cause all the rest of the guys were pretty hard boiled about everything. Not that it made much difference-but when we left New York, it was the first time he had been away from home, just out of school like me, he got awful homesick, and naturally quite seasick, even when we were along side of the dock so when I saw him moping around about ready to cry, I gave him quite a bawling out, not realizing at the time what I was saying or how it would sound to him. At any rate, he thought I was some sort of a god I guess, and after that he was pretty friendly. He had been used to kicking when he didn't feel good, wouldn't try to move a 150 pound sack of sugar or anything, but he soon snapped out of it, and we got along fine."

Kearny traveled from Newark, through the Panama Canal and up the West Coast on the *Sunugentco*. How did he get to the ship? In the leather pouch that we call "Daddy's wallet" is a copy of a telegram from September 30, 1925, now falling to pieces, that let the family know he'd arrived in Newark to join the ship. "Return sailing date indefinite. Hope things are ok at home. Bus ride to Newark roughest part of trip."

He would be home in time to sign up for the National Guard in March, 1926. He would be home in time to start an apprenticeship in the print shop. He would be home in time to attend his mother's funeral.

ॐ

The mere possession of type does not make a typographer any more than [possession of] paint makes an artist.

– Lessons in Printing

In the early days of printing, when every line was set by hand, there were type-setting tournaments among printers in the composing rooms of large newspapers. A crowd would gather about the competitors, place their bets, and a race would be on. In 1870 in New York, one famous printing compositor, George Arensberg, won by setting the equivalent of five pages of modern typescript in an hour, letter by letter. In those days a typesetter with a union card, a composing stick and an apron could travel the country as he chose, confident that he could pick up a job in any composing room— a practice called tramping. Tramping was considered a respectable way of life, though some itinerant printers got a reputation for drinking up their paychecks and skipping out. But they could always move on and find another job.

My father would try tramping in 1929, while still an apprentice.

ॐ

The invention of the Linotype cut into the world of compositors and competitions. In one corner of my father's shop there were cabinets full of type faces in a different kind of metal drawer – the fonts for the Linotype, an automatic type-setting and type-casting machine. I can still see it.

The machine looks like a mechanical monster threatening to eat up its operator, who sits at a keyboard, small and low relative to the machine with its top-heavy banks of fonts. It is my father in that huddled chair and as his keyboard clicks, he is surrounded by the sounds of wheels, pulleys and moving metal. Bits of cast metal fall into the machine's stick. The smell of hot metal from the machine's pot is unmistakable. I can see him examining the line of matrices, molds of letters, rearranging two here, removing one there, adding or removing spacers. The half-page of copy he is working on is clipped onto a board just above the keyboard. The Linotype, whose adoption soon reduced the need for hand compositors, casts a slug for each line of type as the operator completes it, then distributes the type back into its case, which provides the most satisfying of the machine's musical sounds as the matrices rise up on spiraling trolleys and fall back into their type case slots in a chorus of descending clicks.

꙰

The dutiful son came home from the sea. For now, the summer of 1926, Kearny was home and embarked on an apprenticeship in his father's business. His mother had seemed well as she posed for the camera on an outing with friends on a stern-wheeler river boat. The group of similarly be-hatted ladies stood in front of the wheelhouse and Marie smiled as she clutched a bouquet of pansies. She took to her bed soon after.

Jack, who had been in school at Stanford, was called back to join Kearny at their mother's bedside in November. Her affliction—uterine cancer.

While she lingered, the boys, as they were still called, went—or were sent—to Portland for an Armistice Day college football game (OAC vs USC) and an overnight stay with their aunt and uncle in Portland.[7] Marie died on November 19, 1926. The notice of the sons' football excursion appeared in the same issue of the *Grays Harbor Post* as the brief obituary dictated by J.W., which he titled, "A gentle spirit passes."

He wasn't there when she died. And he had lost his mother a second time.

---

[7] Presumably Oregon Agricultural College, which later became Oregon State University.

Kearny and Toscar in the Chrysler roadster

The Runaway

Just when it got too dark to see anything but the Milky Way...both tires on the right side of car blew...
—Kearny Clark, from El Paso, 1929

Only one road trip made it into the black pages of our scrapbook, a 1929 outing that looks charmingly old-fashioned. It is the "tramping" trip in the Chrysler roadster that my father talked about sometimes, recalling busy freight yards, bed bugs in El Paso, "Tia Juana." I always imagined it as a great adventure: my father and three others starring in tiny black and white snapshots. They stand around his open car; a couple smiles from the rumble seat; three men pose in front of the Tijuana brewery; a tall cactus dwarfs two figures; my father in a three-piece suit tries to loosen lug bolts; a concrete dam, a mountain road. I wonder who are these people and why was my father driving around so far from home?

I knew he'd sent letters to his girlfriend while he was gone. My sister and I came across a couple of them some years ago and Kristine was struck by the tenor of the writing, the mind-set of the author:

"It was there all along. The melancholy."

❧

A tidy packet of letters tied with grocery string turned up in the bottom of one of Mother's cardboard boxes. Buttery cream envelopes addressed by typewriter to Miss Dorothy Nielsen—who went by Pete—two-cent cancelled stamps with many different postmarks, a folded page or two of dense typescript in each. Many letters began in the middle of the page, because the writer was accustomed to standard print shop half-sheet copy He folded the page in half, then reversed it, then folded it inside out, always rolling the sheet fold-first into the typewriter and typing until the paper fell out. The effect is a bit topsy turvy. There are xxxed-out words and overstrikes, and words running together and simplified spellings and 1920s slang. The postmarks are useful, since dates on the letter are more casual than clarifying: "Friday nite, 9:00," for example. Most letters close with a simple, "I remain, Kearny" or "KC" or just "Kearny." Once he closes with, "Bon Ami, Dutch Cleanser, Lux, Kearny." Never the elusive, "Love."

These are my father's "love letters," evidence of a long-distance courtship. Except for the wayward one or two my sister found, I didn't see them until both parents were gone. Happy to have them, I tucked them away thinking they would provide clues to my father's aspirations, dreams, feelings for his girlfriend, his life. I thought they might explain why he went away, and what persuaded him to came back.

The family archive also preserved letters he received from his brother, aunt, and father during his travels. He must have been the one to save these, but the collection included only one postcard from the young woman to whom he wrote so faithfully. I recall Mother saying her letters embarrassed her; they were too full of high school silliness, "too sappy." When she bundled his letters together, she threw hers away.

My father grew up in a family that valued books and writing. His father's library was large and eclectic. J.W. Clark took pleasure in reciting long poems from memory, many of them by Tennyson. He wrote pithy editorials and muckraking news articles and personal travel journals for the *Grays Harbor Post*. My father's writing in the letters that have survived strikes me as juvenile, insecure, a bit rough. Of necessity, later he would learn to write a coherent, if somewhat folksy, essay for an editorial. But in winter 1929, some three years out of high school, without the benefit of college, he was inexperienced and he was writing for a small, presumably sympathetic, audience. He had no inkling that someday his children or grandchildren would find them or want to read them.

☙

From his first letters, imagine the scene: Late one cold Saturday afternoon in January 1929, Kearny Clark slings a small Gladstone bag, his portable typewriter, and a trombone into the rumble seat of his roadster, which he'd named "Audrey." That morning he'd taken his girlfriend out for "that one last little spin," and she'd given him a scarf and made him promise to wear it in Paris or Berlin or wherever he went. His printer's apron and composing stick were tucked away in his bag. He tells his Dad's cook to give his dog, Toscar, a treat after he leaves and heads down the driveway. He is twenty years old, an apprentice printer, a fellow getting away. Instead of stopping at K Street to see his girl, he continues downtown past the print shop, crosses the bridge over the Wishkah, and heads east on the only highway out of this coastal lumber town. Twenty miles out he veers south on the cutoff to Centralia. Except for a bowl of soup for warmth in Kelso, he doesn't stop until Portland, where he pulls up at the house of his aunt and uncle and rings the bell. If they are surprised to see him, they are too polite to say so. Here is their young nephew in his sporty Chrysler roadster with six wire wheels. Of course they welcome him.

☙

Later he wrote to Pete, "Boy, I didn't want to go...." In another letter he recalled, "It almost broke my heart to see how my dad took it when I told him I was leaving. I guess he didn't like it, but then I am not going to be gone forever, unless nobody wants me to come back...in about two days you will forget you ever knew me and it is just as well. I want you to have all the fun you can this coming last six months of school."

He mentioned feeling self-pity, feeling blue, not wanting his girl "to feel you're living with a sort of failure."

Was he running away from himself?

☙

When he arrived in San Francisco, he moved in with his friend Bob Cantwell, who was living in a small apartment with his brother Jim, an artist, and Jim's wife, Fanny. Earlier, in Aberdeen, it was Cantwell's sister, also a Dorothy, who introduced Kearny to her good friend "Pete," (Dorothy Nielsen). Bob had come to "Frisco" three months before, when fire closed the plywood mill where he worked in Aberdeen. Bob had written to Kearny that he yearned "for some of the old bull fests we used to enjoy....That's about all we miss in Aberdeen, the folks, and the beer and Mother's cooking." Bob also recalled being driven about the county in Kearny's car, "singing *When Day is Done*, with special attention to the muted [horn] effects." Bob had warned Kearny that the apartment was tiny, and they were eating only "omlets, alternating with macaroni and cheese alternating with scalloped potatoes and omlets again...[and] black coffee." But Kearny was welcomed into the *menage* and began looking for a job.

Letters went back and forth. Pete apparently gushed about high school, where she was a senior, and told him she was waiting for him to come back. He expressed pleasure in getting her letters, but said he was going to stick it out "for many moons to come." Sometimes he encouraged her to find another fellow, sometimes he expressed fear of being displaced, likening himself to Lord Tennyson's Enoch Arden, who, after being lost at sea for years, came home unobserved, only to find his wife remarried and seemingly happy. Arden died nearby, a lost and forgotten man.

ॐ

I admire my father's gumption to set out on his own, given how insecure he felt. He was taking big risks trying to set himself up in a new city. He found that "Hoover's big prosperity is the bunk," noting that few job shops were hiring. In order to get a job he had to persuade himself that he was worthy of getting the job, any job, and then sell himself to an employer, exposing himself to rejection at every turn. Perhaps it helped that he had worked on a freighter; he always held that option in his back pocket. If something didn't pan out soon, he wrote, he'd put his car in storage, send Pete the claim check, and ship out. As long as he was on the coast, the possibility comforted him. If his goal was to pass the time until she graduated, apparently either a job or a posting on a ship would serve.

He had a second goal. In the bottom of his valise were several *Lessons in Printing*. He had completed only four lessons of the first unit before he left home. Lessons I-5 and I-6 were waiting under his neatly folded shirts. Until he completed the program, his apprentice card was all he had to show an employer. At least it showed he had a familiarity with a print shop and printing presses and he wasn't afraid of getting ink on his hands.

In his love letters he admitted he had a problem with authority. On a number of occasions he had encounters with the law and mentioned getting mad and arguing with a cop, convincing himself that all cops were "terribly dumb."

His father badgered him about coming home and his aunt assured him he was everybody's favorite. He wrote about college men and at one point suggested he should finish the *Lessons in Printing* and try to work his way through college. Apparently he never mentioned this desire to his father, or got any encouragement from him in that direction. But Kearny would go to great lengths to help his Cantwell friends, who took him in when he ran away.

ॐ

After a few weeks' search, he found a job as a pressman for a newspaper in Larkspur, a small town nestled between a redwood forest and the Corte Madera slough, just north of Sausalito in Marin County. He would set up housekeeping in a tiny room near the print shop. This called for a celebration before he left San Francisco. He and the Cantwells wanted to "raise ned tonite, the only restriction being that no one spends any money." I can picture the scene from details in his letters:

A small furnished apartment on Leavenworth Street with a Murphy bed, a Pullman kitchen, an unheated communal bathroom out in the hall with a too-small bathtub. Bob with a pad of paper, Kearny at his portable typewriter, Jim at his drawing board, Fanny making coffee and reading *Cosmopolitan*. If Bob has commandeered the only table, Kearny probably sits on the floor with his Corona on his lap. They take turns putting a record on the turntable. Jim is working on illustrations for a client in New York. Bob is writing sophisticated short stories, hoping to break into the East Coast literary world. Kearny is admitting his fear of becoming Enoch Arden and at the same time telling his girl to go out and have a good time. His life in Larkspur will be challenging and lonely. He writes in the next letter, "I sure hate myself."

Except for his obvious blue moods, the accounts of young Kearny's travels make entertaining reading. He later took my mother, brother and me to some of the places he mentioned: another apartment with a Murphy bed in a hilly section of San Francisco, a visit with Jim and Fanny Cantwell near there, by then also parents. Memories of our trip as a foursome in 1939 reassure me that the lonesome traveler did return home, finish his lessons, and marry that Gal Sal who saved every one of his letters.

ॐ

Eight weeks after leaving home, four of the weeks spent working long hours as a pressman for little money and living alone in a basement room in Larkspur, Kearny felt ready to move on. The Cantwells had received word that they needed to stake out a place in Arizona for the sake of a younger brother, ill with tuberculosis. Kearny wrote Pete, "This job and all has been kinda tough, and I sure will be glad to be on my way with Bob. He sure is a good kid, and I know of no other person I would rather travel with than he."

Though the first plan was that Bob and Kearny would leave, when they actually drove away from San Francisco, the car was full: Bob's brother and sister-in-law surrendered the apartment and their jobs and came along. "You can well imagine what a load my poor car is carrying with all the luggage, and human freight too. The springs are on a level keel, and the slightest bump touches the axle, so at 50 miles [per hour] I sure gotta pick the road with the most discreet and intensive care."

A photo in his album comes to life in his next letter to Pete. "It must be a strange-looking spectacle our outfit presents, with a muddy, dusty roadster, top down, baggage weighting it down to the fenders, all four occupants bespectacled, two of them looking like hooded terrors [Jim and Bob in leather aviator helmets], one with hair blown and tangled, and a very dainty looking young lady in their midst, all moving along as fast as the law and the roads permit." They were getting sunburned "something fierce," wrote the young Kearny, who was pleased with the newfangled "colored" sunglasses and whose narrative skills were improving.

He sounds willing to abandon his hard-to-get job and take up the burden of his Cantwell friends. Their obligation to their brother was obvious. Kearny agreed to become a member of the family for the duration of their Arizona campaign because his friends needed a car.

"The outfit" planned to drive to Phoenix by way of Los Angeles, hoping in LA to get near enough to Fatty Arbuckle's Plantation Road House to hear Red Nichols' orchestra. They meant to sneak in or listen through a window. "We may not be able to find the place but it is some incentive to have fun, and that is the best way to do anything [even] if it is only going to a funeral." He never mentioned whether they got within earshot of Arbuckle's place, but describes another scene as they traveled:

Bob "sits in the rumble seat en route, and has a watch, several maps, this typewriter, and a good imagination, and writes a log of our trip as we go. We got a bunch of telegram blanks, and he has been filling them out and sending them home on the way....He is also general bookkeeper, accountant and secretary of the expedition." Kearny has a camera and takes the snapshots that survive: "the outfit" in front of breweries in Tijuana, Fanny in the midst of the luggage holding a small whisky bottle, an auto court, my father in a tree holding a sign. In a very short time they decide Los Angeles "isn't much of a place." In LA's hot weather Kearny finds that if he goes too fast his car "gets up steam and that little green ball turns red...it takes all kind of engineering" to keep the car going smoothly. Fortunately, Kearny has a knack for fixing mechanical devices, whether a typewriter, a printing press, a two-toned horn or an internal combustion engine. He keeps his "buss" in running shape.

They took a day's detour to San Diego and "Tia Juana" where, free of Prohibition laws, they were overwhelmed by the free flow of booze, and where Kearny met some aggressive cops on the return border crossing. "Gee honey...Tia Juana IS different," he wrote. "Boy, one beer after another, and then some more, to say nothing of scotch and bourbon, etc. I sure made a pig out of myself, but it's the first real drinking I've enjoyed since New Years Eve, and I guess that the lack of anything goes for extremes when the chance offers itself, hence my present state of illumination."

On returning to the U.S. side of the border, my father was stopped and found himself challenged "to prove my ability and sobriety to drive on to the land of the free and the home of the brave. They asked me if I had had anything to drink, and being the boy scout I am, I told them yes, two or three beers." The outfit was well dressed. Kearny was wearing a three-piece tweed suit and tie, but he thought his terribly sunburned nose hadn't helped his case, and he was asked to demonstrate "marching on straight lines, and standing with my feet and toes together and closing my eyes, etc." But they let him go on. "Boy I was sure sore, but what can a poor guy do? That wasn't all. While I was in Tia Juana, we were all driving around taking pictures of brewery signs, etc. and I managed to excite the ire of a Mexican policeman." Kearny then summarized in detail his history of being bawled out by cops, a numbered list that was getting longer the further he got from home. A strange way to impress a girlfriend.

"So, MYGALSAL, you are right when you say I must have a cop complex. Still lots of road to Phoenix, and I will no doubt add to my record, enviable that it now is."

ल

A silver-striped Nordstrom gift box labeled "Daddy's wallet" sits on top of my goldenrod-colored file cabinet. It shelters the soft leather pouch, a smaller wallet, and my father's leather key case containing many keys snapped into metal hooks: keys for several cars, a house, and the doors of the shop. I surprise myself by questioning whether I still need to preserve such items, especially those keys that once opened cars long since junked, a shop whose building has succumbed to the wrecking balls, a home given over to a series of new owners.

Among the seemingly random papers in the pouch are four thumbnail photos of my father that must have been taken in a photo booth. Elsewhere I found a larger signed photo in a Photomaton Studios folder. The unusual thing in all these photos is that the subject is wearing a scarf. I don't recall ever seeing my father wear a scarf. It must be the one Pete gave him before he left home, to wear in Paris, she said, or wherever his travels would take him.

Automated photo "studios" swept the country in the late twenties and were conveniently placed in arcades, amusement parks, fairs and bus depots. For twenty-five cents, the user got a strip of eight small photos in eight minutes and could pay extra for folders, frames, and obviously, enlargements.

The slightly out-of-focus larger print is the last formal photo any of us have of my father —I'm not counting the mug shot taken at Steilacoom in 1962, though it, too, is formal. I hadn't remembered what a wide grin he had. That might explain why it felt so wonderful when he smiled, like a gentle sun shining down on you. He looks, he was, older by four years, and more mature than in his sober-faced and better-focused high school graduation pictures.

I imagine the scene at the Photomaton booth. The young man in a suit and tie enters a tiny cubicle, drapes the scarf along the lapels of his jacket, tries to straighten his tie, perches on the bench, and feels silly as he waits for the camera's snap. He growls a bit, talking to a friend, *flash*; he looks up at a fly on the wall, giving a nice profile, *flash*. His friend makes a joke, he laughs, *flash*. The friend says, wipe that grin off your face, *flash*. He finally relaxes and gives the opening a full smiling face, looking as confident as Bing Crosby, *flash*. He asks the operator to make a larger copy of that last one and blushes when the guy asks, is that for your girl? He goes to a stationery shop to buy a large envelope, carefully signs the print, and sends it off in the mail. My guess is that this scene took place in early 1929 in the Ferry Building at the foot of Market Street in San Francisco. He had no idea when he would turn his roadster north to follow that photo home.

❧

In his next letter, he lamented that he was now 2,000 miles from home. He tried to say things about Dorothy's life in high school, though it was seeming remote to him by then, since further letters from Pete, if any, must have been chasing his forwarding instructions.

After the detour into Tijuana, the group drove on to Phoenix, which, he wrote, is "about the hottest sunniest driest place I ever hope to have the pleasure of being in...[it] is sure some town. Right in the middle of a desert, lots of Indians, Mexicans and Negroes to say nothing of...tourists. Sure going to be a new experience for Mrs. Cantwell...to come down here and live alongside...others suffering from poor lungs. And the heat!" He reported that the city is about the size of Tacoma, [Washington], "but lots prettier."

ॐ

The four friends settled into an auto camp near the Capitol in "the confines of one small shack." Bob helped Jim find a job painting road signs advertising a grocery store. Kearny applied for a job in a big printing shop. He wrote more about Phoenix: "There are 60,000 people living here at flood. Flood means in the winter time, 'cause in the summer it gets so hot that everyone with money enough moves out to a place where there is enough cool to sleep." Air conditioning was rare in 1929.

After peeling and eating a raw onion, he described their living situation. "Jim says we are all deteriorating in the tropics, and to see the room we live in you would think so. In order to make room for all the unpainted signs, etc., everything including the chair (singular) is piled on the bed. I am sitting on the rumble seat cushion now, and the [typing] machine is resting on its reputation...days are awfully dry and dusty but the nites are quite cool and clear and seem too nice to have to waste as they are being wasted.

"Being an idle loafer the last week has pointed out the fine fun a fellow can have with a little dough and lots of spare time, but that is all, as our only possession since leaving Frisco has been time." Their life style was abstemious—"Jim and Bob smoke Bull Durham, or cut Lucky Strikes in two and smoke one half at a time. Whenever we sit down to eat the beans or hash, someone mentions fresh strawberries and ice cream, and then we all chip in and picture a most marvelous meal, after which we return to the beans and try to be content."

Kearny mentioned a steam-fitter who lived in the cottage next to them, who gave them some one-day-old homebrew, the first alcohol they'd had since Tijuana, "More sickening than anything else." The neighbor used to work in Aberdeen "and wanted to talk to us about the country around Grays Harbor." Everyone was homesick. "Jim is playing his uke, Bob is softly singing along as a train pulled by. A big 'compound' locomotive goes past our window. The track is only about 100 feet from our house and every time a train goes by, the windows rattle and the doors shake." He was not complaining about the trains; years later during the war, he would often take his second daughter down to stand next to the tracks in Aberdeen when the evening train came in, just to feel those rattles and shakes in his bones, and quiver with the whistles and perhaps remember his days on the road.

Kearny and Bob accepted jobs as bus boys in a cafeteria, which lasted only until Kearny got in a fight with the owner's mother, "who thinks she is some sort of a boss. Anyhow, I quit, and Bob quit too....That is the first time I have ever quit a job in a real heat. Once I get started I got no diplomacy...."

Fairly soon Kearny reported that Phoenix had become "a hick town." The handyman job he'd scrounged didn't pay enough "to buy decent victuals." When Jim got "a slick job" in Phoenix as "an artist of some sort," Bob and Kearny were free to move further east, Bob to a pipeline job in the desert, and Kearny to a job in the pressroom of a newspaper plant in El Paso. He again set up housekeeping in a tiny room: "Picture me—All alone, in an auto camp, writing in my negligee so to speak, with nothing but an inspiration to make me go on. I said all alone, but it's not so. Here, propped up among some peanut butter, mayonnaise, salt, coffee, sugar, paring knife and a thermos bottle, sits the picture of 'My Gal Sal.' I can't help but grin when I look at the whimsical smile on the countenance of the subject, and a grin is worth quite a good deal in the present state of affairs." If this was her yearbook photo, he was admiring the face of a wholesome young woman framed in a flapper's bob, with only a hint of a smile—she was self-conscious about her bad teeth—projecting a calm and optimistic outlook.

He had received back pay from his last National Guard service, which put real money in his pocket. He wrote that he had "practically decided to go [back] to Fort Worden, if I can live to get there. I hate to go back home in some respects, but it is the place for me. I should never have left my dad or my dog, and I only can hope I ain't done wrong by anyone." He didn't mention his girl. I don't know what she was telling him in the missing letters. I wonder whether it bothered her to be left off that list.

As he got ready to leave he talked about the place: "This El Paso is kinda of a rum joint...quite a hick town, but there is lots of railroading, and a smelter and sawmills, is really a pretty live place. Ciudad Juarez, just across the Rio Grande, affords one all the conveniences of Tia Juana. Bob and I went over there yesterday and *looked* around. One beer, one cheese sandwich, and one apple apiece was our total dissipation, and altogether, we decided it was too much. This is too hot, and dry a place to indulge in alcoholic beverages." They saw "a bunch of Mexican Rebels over in Juarez. One poor guy was so loaded down with bullets, and a rifle he could hardly navigate."

He signed off the letter saying he needed to "take a nap before beating it down to my job, or position, as some college men would prefer to have their endeavors labeled." He asked "What is the date of [your] Graduation?"

While Bob Cantwell was working in the desert north of El Paso, he got the acceptance letter that changed his life and ended Kearny's sojourn. Bob's friend Calvin Fixx, in spite of having to hock his typewriter every few months to survive in New York City, had typed up Bob's stories nicely and shopped them around among the people he met as a stenographer for a literary agent. The letter was signed by Lewis Mumford and two other editors. Cantwell's story "Hanging by My Thumbs" was to be published in *The New American Caravan* volume of 1929, among works by Erskine Caldwell, e e cummings, Stanley J. Kunitz, Joseph Mitchell, and other established writers. Kearny may not have realized what a distinction this was for Bob. It pleases me that my father was close to a man aspiring to become a literary writer. In high school, I read the biography of Nathaniel Hawthorne that Cantwell wrote later, and I've since read and admired his two radical proletarian novels set in a Northwest town that felt like Aberdeen. What my father appreciated about him was his conversion from radical leftist to Republican views and his long career as an editor for *Time* and *Sports Illustrated*.

Kearny and Bob headed home.

Association with Bob Cantwell, and Jim and Fanny, had gotten Kearny through a hard time, a time when he had lost his confidence, when he was feeling sorry for himself. He appreciated their help early on: "They sure were great friends to me when I hit Frisco last January. No telling where I'd be now." In correspondence with Bob, Calvin Fixx had written: "That Kearny is a pretty damn fine guy. He has all my respect, and if that kind of devotion means nothing then God help the rest of us poor bastards." But writing from his National Guard duty at Fort Worden that June, Kearny told Pete he was glad to have left them [the Cantwells] behind: "It's kinda like a responsibility to look out for them."

A recurrent theme in Cantwell's short stories was, in the words of a later reviewer, that "happiness is achieved only after one has gained some instinctive knowledge of his own...[and developed] individual accountability and personal responsibility for action."[8]

After more than four months on the road supporting himself and giving a lot of help to his friends, Kearny must have gained some of the knowledge Bob wrote about. Though not yet committed to having a *fiancée*, he was still writing to Pete. He felt drawn back to the big gun he got to shoot on Guard duty. He may have come to realize that the freedom of the open road came at the price of loneliness. That even on the road he couldn't get away from his father.

Or from himself.

---

[8] John M. Vermillion, Robert Cantwell, *Dictionary of Literary Biography*, Vol 9. American Novelists, 1910-1945, Part I. Bruccoli Clark, 1981. Gale Research Book Co.

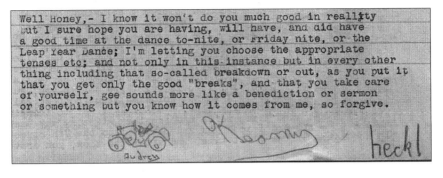

Well Honey,- I know it won't do you much good in reallity
but I sure hope you are having, will have, and did have
a good time at the dance to-nite, or friday nite, or the
Leap Year Dance; I'm letting you choose the appropriate
tenses etc; and not only in this instance but in every other
thing including that so-called breakdown or out, as you put it
that you get only the good "breaks", and that you take care
of yourself, gee sounds more like a benediction or sermon
or something but you know how it comes from me, so forgive.

Audrey

Kearny

heck!

Excerpt from a letter from Kearny Clark to his Gal Sal, March 1929
with sketch of his roadster, Audrey

Humoring the Boss

So, we are two of a kind, each independent and capable of going his own way but I want our ways, yours and mine, to travel parallel for a time.
—J.W. Clark, letter to Kearny, 1929

J.W. had not been happy when Kearny left and wrote him many fatherly letters signed either "Sincerely, 'Dad'" or "Your affectionate, 'Dad.'" It seems fitting that the Dad is in quotes since Kearny and Jack always referred to their father as "The Boss" or, out of his hearing, "The Old Man." Until his stenographer Anna quit for a better job, his letters came neatly typed on yellow Quick Print Co. stationery. Early on J.W. urged Kearny to stay away as long as he was enjoying it and to call on his Dad if he needed money, offering to send some of his own "that you can use any old time," or to send Kearny's cash in twenty-dollar gold coins that he'd left in the safe. "Don't try to go to work too soon, you haven't had a vacation in the Lord knows how long, a month's loaf wouldn't hurt you a bit."

After a month or so, J.W. started to remind Kearny that "you have your old job here and your home on the hill, a sheet anchor to windward that'll hold if a gale comes." By March he expressed the endearingly visual sentiment that "we will all be glad when we receive word that you have turned the prow of the dandy little Chrysler in this direction."

J.W. was concerned to hear that Kearny was doing his own cooking in limited circumstances. "Don't know how that batching stuff will work on a man's stomach. I think if I had to batch I would buy a Jap or something." J.W.'s cook was not a "Jap," but a woman from the South Side who came in daily to look after his household, which included sons Jack, Kearny when he was home, and his sister-in-law, Klara.

Kearny's letters to J.W. were more formal than those to Pete because he knew that his father would be sharing them with friends, and as it turned out, anyone J.W. met on the street including Kearny's friends. J.W.

complimented Kearny's "great description of the town and [the] place where you work [Larkspur]...If you desired you could turn your talents to writing as your power of concentration and description makes easy reading." Kearny learned from his Aunt Klara that J.W. held forth at social occasions by reading from his letters.

Kearny had felt a lot of tension before he left when the old man was in the house; his letters had mentioned finding it hard to make moonshine or listen to his own music.

When Kearny wrote that he would probably come back for his National Guard duty, J.W. was delighted. "Any man that can win the efficiency cup of Battery "A" [as Kearny had the previous year] is too good a soldier to lose from the company, and Battery "A" isn't the only place you fit in in Aberdeen.... You have demonstrated that you can go into a strange land and hold your own and that makes every man feel good."

Later J.W. noted that the cook, as well as his dog, who goes out hunting for him, wished Kearny would come back. "You have done pretty well to stay on the job as the country is full of idle men in all lines." He was also proud that his youngest son did "not waste" his money and told about "old constable Hopkins" coming in to garnish wages against Moore, their pressman, "a first-class workman...but he just can't take care of his own affairs."

He offered, more than once, to send Kearny a package: "Wouldn't you like the little portable Victrola and a bunch of the records sent down to you?" Kearny declined, realizing if he was going to help the Cantwells he needed to travel light. And perhaps he wanted to maintain his independence a while longer.

In passing, J.W. wrote, "I wish that you and I could make a trip to Africa and while we wouldn't try to kill as much game as [his friend] Bill [Lowry] did, we would have a swell time." In the next letter, hearing that Kearny was going to drive the Cantwells to Phoenix, J.W. warned that the terrain would not look like Washington: "To look across plains without trees will be a new experience and will fit you for the trip you and I will take sometime to Dakota." Clearly J.W. had no idea what rugged desert country looked like, nor how little it resembles the plains of the upper Midwest. Kearny wrote back with vivid descriptions of "a wild...desert, mountain country...narrow [miles] wind[ing] uphill and down" on the

Apache Trail—now a Scenic Route from Phoenix to Globe on the way to El Paso—that J.W. proudly published in the *Post*.

J.W. stuck a twenty-dollar bill in a letter and wrote, *"Don't you send it back*. I know that you can make your own fight...but once in a while 'when a feller needs a friend' it's good to know that such a guy exists. I merely want you to feel that way when you think of me. You are now a man and can make your fight even as I." Kearny "kicked" about the twenty, but decided to keep it "in trust." It is doubtful that Kearny told J.W. about the lean pickings in the rustic cabin in that auto camp in Phoenix, but J.W. may have guessed it.

He noted that Kearny was in the "country that was taken from the Mexicans by General Phil Kearny," and recounted the history of General Kearny's campaigns and his part in the conquest of Arizona and southern California. "So you see, my boy, you're in the land where one of your ancestors traveled, the man after whom you are named. Like you he was not afraid of traveling in a strange land and this is not what Jack calls Hooey."

Talking about Kearny's schoolmate Bob Forbes, who enlivened evenings on the local radio station, J.W. admitted, "I have never learned to use the radio and am therefore denied the pleasure of hearing Bob." Aunt Klara wrote the same lament; apparently it was only the youngest, Kearny, who knew how to tune the newfangled thing.

ॐ

When stenographer Anna went to work for an insurance company, J.W. had to resort to longhand. His script is large and readable, with even larger, more flowery capitals and graceful crossings of the tees that look like gentle waves on an ocean of words. When he had installed a new steno, he dictated to her: "The loss of Anna was not irreparable and that is true of any woman. You can always find another which is encouraging." One wonders what her replacement, the "skinny little thing" who "does good work," thought as she typed this statement? Had J.W. felt so little for Marie?

"I would be glad to hear that you will turn the prow of the Chrysler this way....If you still want to work at something other than printing you can find work in this Northwest. I don't want to advise you to do anything distasteful to you." When he sent along another twenty dollar bill, he wrote "I have no other pal and I want you to let me be one to you."

By April J.W. was openly urging Kearny to come back home. He sent the twenty-fifth anniversary issue of the *Post* and the first issue of Volume 26. He also admitted he was studying rifle catalogues, hoping to go to Alaska the latter part of August to "see how it feels to look a Kodiak in the face. I have always wanted the Alaska trip and the chance now occurs. I want to get a gun heavy enough to stop one of the big fellows, which are the largest animals that grow on this half of the globe. They are supposed to be somewhat rough."

J.W. and Kearny never made a trip together to Dakota or to Africa. It is heartbreaking to think that my grandfather was so eager to get his youngest son back home that he held out the prospect of the things that he, J.W., considered desirable. And that he didn't realize how crowded his son must have felt, how difficult it might have been for his son, whether or not wanting to hunt, to travel with him. Apparently Kearny couldn't ask for what he really wanted, a chance at college.

ॐ

His brother Jack wrote to Kearny, "What the hell! Why be a $50 a week man for $20....Get wise to yourself and throw a monkey wrench in the press," on learning how Kearny felt about his job in Larkspur. Jack warned Kearny not to write him with "all the dope on your Tia Juana trip," because "The Boss has a habit of 'accidentally' opening most of my mail."

Jack's letters to Kearny were undated, brief, and to the point. He sent "his weekly epistle of knowledge, and also enclosed $10 on account." When he had cleared his balance of twenty dollars, "soon the world will be mine."

Kearny wrote about Jack in a letter to Pete: "As to my brother...sometimes he says something which is indisputably true, and proper but as a whole, he is very unreliable and doesn't mean much [of] what he says, so just kinda humor him and someday he will come to and realize what other people think of him, and then he will be all right. He is a good guy in most respects, and a darned good friend to have as long as he doesn't have to borrow money from you."

Though he was fully involved in the family print shop, Jack spent some time that winter with a cousin trying to raise money to manufacture airplanes, an enterprise J.W. disparaged. An enterprise Kearny disapproved of. An enterprise that fizzled. Jack wrote, "Irregardless, I'm about ready to quit the printing business. Am convinced that Father will treat me as a small boy all my life." He suggested he might meet Kearny in Paris on July 4, 1929, or he might pull out for points unknown. He would soon be a "free agent as far as my debts are concerned, and then to hell with it all…"

Jack was taking some interest in their father's social life: "The Boss is sporting around quite a bit these days. Don't know whether he or Klara tell you anything about that angle of his life or not. He's throwing a very private dinner party for six at the Pacific Beach Hotel (45 miles west of town) tonight. I'm not supposed to know anything about it, but things like that do get out. He is right now engaged in dressing himself all up like Rudolph Valentino, or some sheik. Found half a case of Mexican Brandy stored in the basement, not a bottle cracked—so naturally I stayed sober."

Jack was mentally preparing for the possibility of his father marrying again: "There's a fifty-fifty chance of my leaving here, especially if the Boss busts out like I'm afraid he will. He's been giving two or three dames the rush." However, it would not be J.W. who would marry in the coming year, nor would it be Jack. The attentive reader will put his money on Kearny and his Gal Sal.

From Kearny Clark's scrapbook,
a shoot at Fort Worden's Battery Benson

The Guns of Battery Benson

At the command HOME RAM given by the chief of breech the detail rushes
the projectile forward into its seat...the powder-serving detail...[will] place the
nose of the powder tray in the breech recess...
—Coast Artillery Weapons—Service of the Piece

A few years ago my husband and I took our oldest grandchildren to Fort Worden, on the northern coast of Washington's Olympic Peninsula, because I wanted to see this place where my father had camped with the National Guard. I wondered how to prepare them for the experience.

It is one thing to regale your children with stories of your national guard training, about the thrill of shooting the big gun, about standing at attention in the rain, about eating army chow, as my father had. It is another thing to try to convince your grandchildren that a hundred-year-old coast artillery fort will be interesting because their great-grandfather (*who?*), once upon a time (*when?*), was chief of breech and got to shoot a big cannon. But I tried. Neither of these "things" prepares one for the actual experience of setting four pre-teens and a fourteen year old loose in a concrete warren of ancient gun emplacements.

None of the verbal windup matters to them. No association with a great-grandfather or a grandmother's childhood memories piques their interest. That the old fort had some role in defense of the coast, a total snooze. That each of the old guns had a name matters not. That anyone important had ever been there before, not. It doesn't even matter that the guns are gone. What is real and interesting is solid, graffitied concrete all around them, cool and dark and cavernous and hidden and echoey and full of ladders and high platforms and best yet, it feels dangerous.

Our grandchildren would have happily stayed for days probing the concrete labyrinths of Fort Worden.

ɕ

Fort Worden lies just west of Port Townsend and east of Port Angeles where ferries ply the deep waters of the Strait of Juan de Fuca to Vancouver Island and Victoria, B.C. We and the grandchildren were camping our way around the Olympic Peninsula, expecting to join their parents at Pacific Beach in a few days. Clark's children, Hannah, Alex, and Caley from Los Alamos were ten; Stephanie twelve, and Robert, fourteen, lived near my husband and me in Salt Lake City. I had never visited the Fort before and had to quickly bone up on some history.

🍎

My father was barely out of the dresses his mother fancied when the fort was completed in 1912. Fort Worden's defensive gun emplacements dominated the bluff overlooking an important sea passage and represented the height of military technology, as it was understood by the Army's Endicott Board in 1885. The fort was built using nineteenth century methods: pick and shovel, horse-drawn scrapers, a donkey engine hauling supplies from the beach up to the top of the bluff, a network of railroads transporting cement and steel to the site, and huge fixed guns cast in East Coast foundries set up to guard the Strait of Juan de Fuca, at the place where the channel narrowed into Admiralty Inlet. In its prime, prior to The Great War, it was a proud facility for the Coast Artillery division of the Army. Strategically placed in a "triangle of death," with forts on nearby islands, the guns were expected to protect the entry to Puget Sound, Seattle and the naval facilities at Bremerton.

The stationary fortification at Fort Worden was one of our country's largest coastal defense establishments, and, like the others, became obsolete almost as soon as it was completed due to the development of better naval firepower and later of air power. In 1917 the big guns were dismantled, shipped to France, and reassembled on train cars. Officers from Fort Worden, thought to be the best gunners in the Army, taught troops in the field how to use them as mobile heavy artillery. The guns were all returned to their defensive positions soon after that war and were integral in the training of my father's Battery A, 248th Coast Artillery Regiment of the Washington National Guard in the late 1920s. The fort was an active army base until 1953.

🍎

The children won't sit still for a recitation of this fascinating history, I'm sure.

For me, Fort Worden is a beautiful August afternoon, a beach on the northeast corner of the Olympic Peninsula and curiosity about this place that had inspired such bittersweet nostalgia in my father. As I round up five sandy youngsters and help them through a beach shower near the fort's boat dock, I fear we might not have time to see the Coast Artillery Museum and my father's Battery Benson up on the hill. I don't know what I expect to see and feel, what will be left to help me understand his guard experience. But I know the name of his gun battery as well as I know the name of his typing teacher, who also was my typing teacher, and the name of the doctor who delivered me, who was a crony of my grandfather and a retired Army officer who no doubt served for a time at this fort.

My father returned from his southern sojourn of winter and spring 1929 for the June encampment at Fort Worden. His battery hoped to win the year's target shooting competition. He wrote to Pete that he was "holding down Chief of Breech...working on the dang gun." He had been promoted to sergeant, which put him in the top echelon of the battery of three officers and sixty-eight enlisted men.

His Worden story involves military discipline, passing inspections, saying "Yes, sir" and "No, sir," taking his turn at duty in charge of quarters, following protocols for firing the big gun of Battery Benson, and hoping to beat out other batteries.

Benson was one of the last batteries built, and had two 10" guns mounted on disappearing carriages once called the "acme of ingenuity." The carriage had two sets of levers that raised the gun over the edge of the parapet for firing and lowered it behind the concrete wall for loading in relative safety. The battery was built into the hillside and connected by a tunnel to the main batteries of the fort—Ash, Quarles, and Randol—which contained both 10" and 12" guns on barbette carriages that kept them above the edge of the emplacement in plain view of any enemy at all times.

My father relived shooting the gun in a letter to his nine-year-old grandson Clark. My father wrote, "This rifle fired a 10" diameter projectile [that was] 4- or 5-feet long and weighing 517 pounds; we used two big powder bags made of the finest silk and the powder summed up to something like 220-250 lbs. Memory has slipped on that weight, and actually we got the powder down once to 205 lbs., and the recoil mechanism failed and we almost wrecked our big gun. It was exciting, that time, with steel locking pawls sheared off and flying all over the gun emplacement. Some ordnance man had goofed on his slide rule and cut our powder allowance and like saving a nickel it must have cost plenty to renew the broken parts...."

As chief of breech for the 10" gun, my father was apparently responsible for getting everyone clear of the gun, stuffing propellant bags behind the projectile, closing the breech, and holding the cord that fired the small bullet to set off the larger charge that fired the gun. No wonder he wanted to be there for that year's shoot. But it was hard on his hands: "I got a couple of awful looking hands, all yellow from burned powder." Munitions plant workers who had to handle this kind of explosive were called "yellow people." He was lucky only his hands went yellow. I don't recall whether our son appreciated these details at the time, but Clark soon became interested in toy rockets, worked with rocket fuels for an aerospace company, and earned an MS in explosives engineering. My father was right to have written to him about his guard experience.

My father was enjoying his memories: "[The gun] really was a beauty, shooting very accurate, loading extra fast—my job as chief of breech was to direct the loading, see that all safety systems were go as the astronauts call it [he's writing in February 1966], and order the gun tripped into 'Battery' which was its firing position. We would throw the projectile some 16,000 yards, something like 9 miles, at a target only a strong telescope could see. The shell, in the air, was a thriller, sounding like an express train hitting the straight-away at full throttle."

Snapshots in my parents' album show the battery with the gun in both the raised and lowered positions, and one photo captures the jet of flame and smoke being expelled from the barrel of the gun during firing. Another snapshot shows that the gun's barrel could support twenty men. The myth always repeated in coast artillery circles is that no American coastal defense gun was ever "fired in anger." This could mean either that they were a good deterrent or, perhaps, an unnecessary line of defense. Benson's guns were salvaged in 1943 and shipped to Fort Stevens at the mouth of the Columbia River for use as anchors for submarine nets.

My grandfather reported the successful shoot of 1929 on the front page of that week's *Post*—the headline: "Battery A Scores 5 Hits in 7 shots on 10-inch Gun." Two weeks later J.W. published four more photographs, again on page one, with the headline "Big Gallery Watches Battery 'A' of Aberdeen in Action." Accompanying the photographs, a long story, probably written by J.W. and based on Kearny's letters, boasts that his town's battery broke all former records for firing the big guns, and destroyed two twelve-foot targets beyond the five-mile range. The guard group returned home as champions from what was generally agreed to have been "the best camp in the history of the artillery at Worden."

Kearny's twenty-first birthday fell on the day of that big shoot. What a way to celebrate!

❧

Today Fort Worden is a state park where one can camp on the beach or near the Parade Ground, visit the Commander's Quarters and the Coast Artillery Museum, and explore the overgrown coastal defenses on Artillery Hill. Copper Canyon Press is quartered in an old cannon repair shop. The whole area is registered as a National Historic Landmark.

The guns are gone, as are the latches on the heavy steel doors, the apparatus for trolleying ammunition, the carriages for raising and lowering the guns, the elevators and conveyors that brought explosives up from underground storerooms, the countless other mechanical and electrical infrastructure that supported a once-active artillery battery.

What is left is a post-industrial military slum of concrete and rust, mazes of platforms, passageways and underground rooms that attract artists of all kinds, from graffiti experts to fine art photographers—in short, a perfect playground for agile youth. And that is where our grandchildren disappeared, spending a long summer afternoon they hoped would never end.

I sit on the parapet of Battery Benson thinking about what Fort Worden meant to my father. The view of the strait must have been stunning during his tenure. Today a vigorous northwest forest of tall pine, red-trunked madrone, and alder crowds the concrete ramparts on all sides, allowing only glimpses of blue water and distant islands. I'm sure my father enjoyed the natural beauty of Worden's shoreline, the wide strait. I wonder if it was patriotism that drew him into the guard, to join with young men and boys from his town preparing to defend their homeland. Maybe it provided a time of bonding with other men, with his older brother, a way to gain approval from them, from the officers. Because the shoot was a success it certainly earned him the respect of his demanding father. But he was still unsure of his place in life.

As I wander around Benson's rough concrete ramparts and platforms, I try to visualize the gun, the loading crew, the human chain trolleying enormous shells to the barrel. I can almost see my father's yellow-stained hands rapidly turning the crank to close the breech and setting off the charge. A Boeing 747 roars overhead, heading westward, and I cover my ears. I would not want to have been close when the gun fired. I am awed that the men would shrug off the blast, crank down the gun, swab out the barrel, and go through it all again, moving as fast as they could without being reckless. They could put the gun through its paces in a matter of seconds. No wonder my father was proud of his guard service.

In the passages behind the gun platform, narrow stairs lead down to interior passageways that seem to go off in every direction. Stumbling through the darkness of one of these, while shouting children elbow by in the other direction, I come to a large vault-like room that echoes like the basement playroom of my grade school, where the girls played Mother-May-I and hopscotch on rainy days. The dust on the floor shows the same pattern of running feet, and the room is just as gloomy. During my father's drills, this had been an ammunition storage vault. Strange drawings and scrawled words look out from the blackened walls. I enter a passageway on the far side of the room, hoping to find my way back to the security and fresh air of the outside world. At a dark corner I sense a figure lurking nearby, and startle even so, even as I recognize the voice of a grandson rasping in his best imitation of Tolkien's Gollum, "There you are, my pre-e-cious!"

Display ad sketched by Kearny Clark
in a "love letter," 1929

cA Roman Holiday

Whenever I get low I think about heading fora big port to scout out another job.
—Kearny Clark, 1929

What kind of a man was my father at twenty-one? Though still telling Kearny what he should do, his dad thought he was competent and reliable, that if dropped on Mars he would soon be running the machinery there. In encounters with traffic cops and highway patrolmen he easily "got sore." He felt cops were laying for him, but also that he might be smarter than they and able to talk them into confusion and out of a citation. He didn't like being bawled out by cops or the typing teacher or the boss's wife. He was sensitive to the opinions of others. At Fort Worden in June, his brother Jack also worked on the big gun. Kearny wrote Pete that "Jack doesn't seem to approve of most of my actions, but he seems pretty friendly most of the time." What is interesting is that he found Jack's apparent disapproval worth mentioning. He'd been relieved to be free of responsibility for the Cantwells. At times he envied seemingly carefree college boys, and thought he might like to be one.

Kearny had been subject to epileptic seizures since he was fourteen, but he never talked about having one, and my mother never mentioned or acknowledged that epilepsy was one of his problems.

His photo album documents the "pretty nice summer" that he had hoped for—going out with Pete for afternoons on the beach, both Pete and Kearny dressed in their Sunday best, smiling for each other, posing with friends, sitting on a blanket next to the portable record player listening to Kearny's favorite music—they visited Pacific Beach and Tokeland—walking together in town after a day of work—she, clerking in a bakery, he an apprentice in his father's print shop.

Because he had reached his majority, his mother's estate was settled in July, three years after her death. Wrinkled and grimy copies of legal papers he kept in his wallet show that she directed the proceeds of the sale of the former Clark home on West Third for the "cost and expenses of maintaining John W. Clark, Jr. in college." (Jack's four years at Stanford.) No mention of money for Kearny's education or other pursuit was listed. There was no other cash in the estate, only real property and shares of stock in Quick Print Co.[9]

J.W. went off alone on a steamer to Alaska to hunt the Kodiak bear. Apparently, once his wayward son returned to the fold, The Boss forgot about his offer of father-son travels. J.W. was gone all of September and October and serialized his account of the trip in the *Post* the next January. The stock market crash that ended the "Roaring Twenties" and signaled the beginning of what came to be called The Great Depression occurred in late October of 1929.

But something else happened in Kearny's world that fall, and he fled again.

༒

In early December Kearny was in Portland, again writing to Pete from his uncle's office, and he had again applied for a job on a freighter, the *West Cactus*. The ship was a sister-freighter to the *Sunugentco* on which he had worked earlier, which, in the reorganization of the Pacific and Dollar Steamship companies, was by then renamed *Admiral Laws*. He was uncertain about whether he would get on the ship, and talked about why he was there: "I don't intend going back to Aberdeen tho, as I figure that by this time my name is pretty well into the dirt on top of making the can the other day, now leaving everything, etc."

A tantalizing statement. He doesn't explain what happened, nor why he was arrested. Presumably Pete, and everyone else in town, knew. Then he wrote, "I cares't [sic] not about anything but your own opinion in the matter and hope to have a letter one day soon to cheer me up."

The *West Cactus* had arrived in Portland that day with a full crew. In the course of the week of loading he expected there would be a couple of vacancies. He said he would like to make this trip "since I started, but that's neither here nor there in the final analysis so to speak, eh wot?"

---

[9]   Several pieces of that real property, tiny lots at Roosevelt Beach and in a Cosmopolis slough, are still in the family, their tax burden still with us after more than a century.

Further on he wrote, "Remember kiddo, I'm with you like anything and all for you to do is say the word, and away we go....I'd like to say lots of things, honey, but wots the use." He signed this letter, "Love, Kearny."

What scurrilous deed had Kearny committed at home that would cause him to think an unskilled job on a freighter was an appropriate penance? Frustrated that I didn't know how to tell this story I went back to my stash of boxes. What had I missed?

In a scrapbook, "School-Fellow Days: A Memory Book" is a receipt dated November 27, 1929 written to Kearny Clark by the Hoquiam Chief of Police. He'd paid a fine of twenty-five dollars for four young men whose names I don't recognize (and himself, presumably). There's a note beside the receipt in my handwriting, written years ago. Until I put my father's letters in order by postmarks and discovered this additional getaway, the receipt hadn't seemed significant. The note quotes my mother, who told me, "Kearny helped these guys burn Hoquiam [high]'s bonfire prematurely, before the Thanksgiving football game."

He felt disgraced for taking part in a childish prank. And for getting caught.

ह

The Turkey Day Classic football game between the high schools of Aberdeen and Hoquiam was (and is) a great example of small town rivalries. With no college or professional team to draw their loyalties, and only one high school, folks in our adjoining towns got excited about the annual face-off, which was inaugurated in 1904. Though his oldest son had played the game, J.W. did not like football. Shortly after his return from Alaska that fall, he wrote a rousing editorial against the sport for "boys of high school age and younger," arguing that "men of that age had not reached their full strength and muscular development." He referred to the game as a "Roman Holiday for howling spectators," and lamented the incidence of "slipped kneecaps, broken ribs and collarbones and still more serious injuries...Just what relation football has to education we have never been able to discover."

When I was in high school twenty-two years later, at the same school my parents attended, I was an enthusiastic fan of high school football. In an editorial for the pre-Thanksgiving issue of the *Ocean Breeze* my senior year, I wrote: "After we devour the mighty Grizzly we will certainly enjoy our turkey dinners. There'll be no danger of indigestion here, for when the

Bobcats clean the Grizzly, they really do it right." Unaware of my father's history, I talked about the pre-game ritual bonfire, a tradition in each of our towns: "John Hoquiam had better put his affairs in order and say his prayers because we are all set to burn him in the rally tonight. After a fair trial the scoundrel has been found guilty of the worst possible crime—that of being a resident of Hoquiam. Tonight we'll be out there to watch him burn, and cheer on the Blue and Gold." That was my view of things in November 1950.

I can imagine how the 1929 bonfire prank happened. After their band practice that Tuesday evening, Kearny, the man with a car, invites some friends for a ride. He loves to motor over the high bridge into Hoquiam. The friends talk about the coming game, and recall the humiliating defeat of the previous year when "touchdown followed touchdown in a regular parade," until Hoquiam had piled up a 70-6 win! One of the guys says, "Let's find someone to beat up." Without thinking, Kearny has driven them to the school and the site of their rivals' waiting bonfire. They are all smokers. Somebody gets out his matches...

That November the Hoquiam fans didn't get to enjoy the flames that were expected to burn Aberdeen's effigy football player. Kearny and his friends found themselves at the station. Fortunately, the police did see it as a prank, levied a small fine, and sent them shamefacedly back across the Hoquiam River. After dropping off his friends, Kearny, his dog at his side, kept driving, all the way to Portland.

It is fascinating that my mother saved the evidence of the prank, going so far as to glue it into the sparsely-populated School-Fellow Days scrapbook.

℩

Though he was on the run again, he was still reaching out to Pete, perhaps hoping she would send a reassuring letter or two and maybe cajole him into giving up his flight. She answered his letter in early December. She also sent him a small box of assorted items from her father's store: "enough stuff...to start a drug store of my own," he wrote. He especially appreciated the cough syrup, her father's own concoction, and the foot powder.[10] Though these things may have been intended for use if he were to ship out, she apparently offered to meet him in Montesano with her "baggage." Montesano, the small

---

[10] The cough syrup was an iodine-based gargle, which was quite soothing; my grandfather's handwritten formulation turned up in my mother's papers.

county seat, was ten miles east of Aberdeen on the way to either Seattle or
Portland.

Kearny's reply rambled and ruminated through the difficulties of his
situation. He felt bad having run out of town with his dog and without
saying goodbye to his dad. "After all he's just about the best friend I got and
I owe him as a son a little consideration....I been making a first class mess
out of everything."

Though still thinking about shipping out, he threw out another idea:
"If I stayed home for 6 months, worked hard on my lessons, and got them
all finished by June—I could start in on the [Linotype] machine, and by
next December, I would get my card, and be all set for the future whatever
that is was or will be. What to do."

He agreed they should meet in Monte "as per 4 o'clock on the corner,
and I'll see you Sunday....Let's make Sunday a turning point, kiddo, hungh?
There is a picture on the wall in my room here [in his uncle's house], the
caption of it is: 'Home-keeping Hearts are Happiest.'"

Encouraged by Pete's response, and prodded by his uncle and host,
who had visited Aberdeen the week after Thanksgiving and reported that
his father was upset by his most recent departure, Kearny went home. He
had missed the family Thanksgiving and knew his recent absence would
draw some comment at the Christmas dinner table. In the formal dining
room on West Sixth Street, after everyone politely spooned bits of canned
fruit cocktail from gold-edged sherbet glasses, J.W. would preside at the
carving of a fragrant golden bird. As was his habit, he would pronounce an
appropriate verse or story with each serving. Kearny's succulent slice of
breast no doubt would come with an allegory about the lost lamb led safely
home by his faithful sheep dog, a black and white collie. Kearny acquiesced
to his father's forceful insistence that his place was in his town, in his
father's house, and in his father's print shop. He could also count on the
adoring and uncritical love of his Gal Sal.

If I had ever asked my mother whether there were ups and downs in
their courtship, she would have dismissed the question. They were madly
in love, she'd say, and just had to find the right time.

On March 30, 1930, J.W. Clark received a telegram from Seattle:
"Married Dorothy [Pete] yesterday. Probably home tomorrow. Kearny."

☙

They had not shared their wedding with either set of parents. Dorothy's mother belittled any boyfriends she knew about and expected her daughters to marry at least a doctor or lawyer. Most of them eloped. Kearny did not yet have his union card. Having taken the plunge, they planned to move into a friend's vacant house. But J.W. insisted that they cancel that plan and live with him.

"That meant we joined a household of 2 bachelors, an ancient Aunt Klara, and us—the lovebirds," she wrote later. I imagine there was some blushing when the newlyweds arrived there that Sunday night. Certainly the new bride would have been bashful, as J. W greeted them and welcomed them into his house. I don't know if Dorothy had visited the home prior to the elopement, but she was surely aware of his strong personality. They would start their new life in Kearny's bachelor quarters, with the record player and records, his school books, his trombone and saxophones, and a twin bed.

J.W. observed all the formalities surrounding a son's marriage; he presented his wife's wedding rings to his new daughter-in-law. She was supposed to call The Boss, "Dad." It was probably he who suggested she sit for a studio portrait that he published in the *Post*. The cheery girl who'd had a "Whoopee time" in high school while her boyfriend was away morphed into a demure matron framed in black cloche, pearls, and a black, fur-collared coat. Gloveless, her folded hands displayed the rings.

I can only imagine the tension in the house between the non-confrontational young bride and the father-in-law, a man accustomed to having his way. My parents would have had to adjust to married life in whispers. They feared that bottles of homebrew they'd stashed in the attic would explode, annoying the Old Man. The bride set about learning to cook. She wrote that the other residents of the house "were accustomed to eating out in restaurants most of the time." Mr. Clark "ate with us several times a week, only when invited, though." She thought it was a strange family: "Four cars—all going to the same shop every day—but each alone."

Within a year, Dorothy gave birth to a son, Philip, and she worried that if he cried in the night he would disturb the household, so "without telling anyone" the young couple moved to a rental house below the hill, taking with them only the twin bed. The following winter the river flooded over the mudflats under the house and baby Philip got pneumonia.

Again, The Boss was not happy, and, in spite of the depressed economy, contracted with an architect and contractor to build a suitable house for his youngest son on a ledge above his own. Building supplies were so scarce, I was told, that in the whole town there was only one set of tile for the face of the fireplace. From the multi-page typed specifications for the construction of the house preserved in Mother's papers I discover that the fireplace installation, with its lovely warm-colored cushions of tile, was one of the very last from the Batchelder shop in Los Angeles. Such fireplaces are much prized today by Arts and Crafts period enthusiasts.

The house was "the only building going on at the time, due to the depression." Mother described the construction, which she visited daily, and noted that "the architect himself...did the staircase posts and the corbels which supported the beam ends. There were 17 kinds of cedar in that beautiful beamed ceiling in the living room and entry halls." The house that she loved and "spent many years taking care of" cost "a bit over $4,000" in 1932.

By the time the house was ready, there had been a premature stillbirth, and I was the new baby when my parents moved back within the Old Man's purview. J.W. had even bought my parents a bedroom set with a double bed.

The next year, J.W. was diagnosed with oral cancer. The absence was beginning. To Kearny it was unthinkable. The Boss had only recently been escorting ladies to the duckblinds of his beloved South Bay Hunt Club. The vigorous outdoorsman who had climbed Mt. Bob in the Olympic Wilderness, hiked trackless Indian territory and Alaskan wilderness, who had been honored as a Tyee Sachem in full Plains Indian headdress because of his trapshooting prowess, the outspoken editor and business man, was going to die.

His illness was so severe and disfiguring that Kearny, who was twenty-six when his father became ill, was not welcome to visit him in the hospital in Seattle. J.W. lingered for almost a year, dying in September 1935. His friend T.M. Quinn provided a tribute to the *Post*'s editor: "In every meeting place and on the editorial page of his cherished paper, his voice and pen trod with iron heel the tender toes of hypocrisy."

His sons wrote a long obituary to accompany a large photo on the front page. Their father had been such a complex creature of learning and masculinity, a man who evoked the bully nature of a Teddy Roosevelt, yet a man who so often had been caught in a snapshot with a toddler in a lacy dress on his knee, or straddling his saddle chair with the youngest son nestled on his lap. In an editorial note, "To our father," his sons wrote: "He lived a life of sincerity, honesty and fidelity. His everyday motto: 'Keep the faith....' He was a real father, but more than that, in the words of a host of his friends, 'He was a man.'"

I like to think that for the graveside eulogy his sons quoted Lord Tennyson's perennial last poem, "Crossing the Bar," which closes,

> *And may there be no sadness of farewell,*
> *When I embark;...*
> *I hope to see my Pilot face to face*
> *When I have crost the bar.*

My mother claimed that Kearny found a way to mention his father every day for the rest of his life.

ॐ

Uncle Jack took over as publisher of the paper and manager of the print shop, while Kearny continued as printer in the back shop. The national economy was improving, and so was the printing business. When the Golden Gate Exposition (we called it the World's Fair), was about to open in San Francisco, Jack, whose wife had just borne a son they named J.W. Clark III, encouraged my father to take a vacation. I look again at the photo taken near my mother's childhood home, the four of us, my parents and Phil and me, looking like we had someplace to go. We were a foursome bound by love, who soon embarked on the happiest of the family's road trips.

.

Kearny and Jack in our front yard, 1940

I shall return...

Last night I saw upon the stair
A little man who wasn't there
He wasn't there again today
Oh, how I wish he'd go away
 —Hughes Mearns, recorded by
 Glenn Miller and Tex Beneke, 1939

The man who wasn't there must have haunted my father every day, starting the day his brother went on active duty. In November 1940, Capt. John W. (Jack) Clark led our town's Marine Reserve unit onto the train, following orders to report to San Diego. Though we were not at war, these men expected to be sent overseas, to bases in the Philippines or one of the "China Stations." Crowds came to the Northern Pacific train station at the foot of Broadway, a band played, and women wept as they said goodbye to husbands or sons. Mother often described how brave Aunt Lil was, how proud we all were of Jack. I imagine my father was silent as he shook his brother's hand in farewell.

En route to the main north-south line, Jack's train passed under what was then the new Tacoma Narrows bridge, the bridge that had earned the name "Galloping Gertie" because of instability in high winds. Just hours after their passage, gale winds whipped the bridge's roadbed in ever-increasing undulations until it twisted, broke apart and fell into Puget Sound. That collapse became part of the family narrative, a harbinger of losses to come.

ॐ

Uncle Jack's impending departure had been a big social event, according to his Aunt Klara's society notes in the *Post*. In his last weeks at home, several of his prominent friends hosted dinners or cocktail parties. I was only seven, but was allowed to attend Aunt Lil's party for him. She was everywhere, passing plates of food, talking to everyone, picking up dirty dishes, napkins, dusting crumbs off the table. Cousin Johnny, a toddler, was passed from arm to arm. Jack flashed his teeth in a silly grin for a friend with a camera, his tweed jacket askew, looking like he hadn't a care in the world.

Jack was the nice kind of tease or practical joker. When his wife Lillian took over my grandfather's house and established house rules, he found imaginative ways to circumvent them. For example, he carefully saved and arranged one square of toilet paper on the empty roll so he wasn't the one who had to replace it.

I remember that Jack wasn't like my father—he was a talker and a storyteller, the kind of man you remembered, and tall. With a long, smooth face and full head of brown hair, he appeared younger than my father. He made people laugh, and he would spin me around in circles. I don't think I ever saw him in his captain's uniform, but I was thrilled by magazine photos of Marines in their full dress regalia and felt proud of my uncle. But mostly I remember him as missing: the uncle who no longer teased me, the husband who wasn't there, the father who wasn't seeing his baby growing into a boy, the brother whose absence challenged my father every day.

☙

On a Friday afternoon at the shop I find my father up on the platform of the folding machine. He flips together the two full sheets of printed newspaper and lets them engage a row of little white rollers; the Rube-Goldberg-like device swallows the sheets, slashes them in half and in half again; the partly folded paper moves sideways, then abruptly down, then sideways again as another blunted blade whacks the next fold. The printed sheets survive moving straps and slashing levers and are spit out in neat stacks of finished papers ready for mailing labels.

The hours I spent standing around as a kid, watching somebody work, and later doing small jobs in the print shop, are among my strongest memories, and now, looking back, gave me a link to my father that just being one of the daughters at home did not.

By the time I was old enough to work at the shop, it had become my father's bailiwick. If one wanted to talk to him, that was the place to do it, as his friends realized. My father was not likely to go out to drum up jobs or drop in on a fellow businessman as Jack had. People had to come to him. There was always a fifth of whiskey in some cubbyhole. If the bottle was empty, the Bright Spot, a tavern I couldn't enter, was just across the street. I'm sure that when he was seated at the bar, a tall draught of beer loosened his tongue.

తె

Jack was among the defenders of Cavite Naval Base in the Philippines when the Japanese attacked Pearl Harbor. We knew that his unit survived the first Japanese air attacks and that he moved with the rest of our troops to the defensive position on the Bataan Peninsula. General MacArthur fled to Australia in March promising that he would return. Jack's last letters as a free man came from Corregidor, where our troops tried to defend the island, at best delaying for a month the Japanese forces' access to Manila Harbor. After Corregidor's surrender in May, we knew Jack, if he was still alive, must be a prisoner of the Japanese, but we heard nothing for months. My father, overwhelmed by having responsibility for his own and his brother's family, was sick with worry about his brother and even thought for a while that *he* would be drafted.

తె

With the North Pacific Ocean just twelve miles by air from Aberdeen, nightly blackouts were ordered starting a week or two after the Pearl Harbor attack. We didn't have shutters or heavy curtains; we just turned out all the lights so the "Japs out there" couldn't see us. In the dark house someone was always tripping over my brother's big shoes, my mother recalled. She took a first aid course and prepared to drive a Red Cross vehicle if there was an emergency. My brother built balsa-wood-and-tissue-paper models of American and Japanese airplanes and Mother studied profiles and models of those in order to be a plane spotter. For the first year of the war she spent Monday nights in a tiny room on the roof of the police station. The spotters boiled water before they made coffee as they would have to do if an attack destroyed the water supply, and they scanned the sky. My father became an air-raid warden and brought home a hard hat, a shovel, and a small water tank with a pump handle and nozzled hose so he could put out fires after a bombing. This scared us for a while, but then we figured out that the tank was good for water fights.

That spring of 1942 our favorite babysitter was hospitalized with tuberculosis. Concerned that I had been infected, Mother took me to the sanatorium in Elma for chest X rays. On every visit I stretched to get my chin on the cold frame of the X-ray machine and heard, "Take a deep breath, and hold it." There was a scar on my lung, but the disease was no longer active. I was allowed to go to school on days my temperature was normal but not allowed to walk, even though it was only a mile. Mornings when I went from the car onto the school grounds, my third-grade teacher, Sister Imelda, invariably greeted me with, "How's poor little Nancy today?"

We had only one car, but we did have ration coupons for gasoline because the shop printed and distributed the ballots for each election. Mother started the day by driving my father to work, then me to school. She brought me home for a hot lunch, then took me back in the afternoon, and brought me home after school. Before dinner we went downtown to pick up my father. If he was still working in the shop, we'd go in. While we waited, my brother Phil walked around the marble stones trying to read what was on the blocks of type. I played with stuff from the scrap barrel or ran in and out of the stockroom. Phil spun around in the swivel chair. Uncle Jack's desk, now my father's, was piled with papers. Mother said it looked like my father was saving all the mail "for Jack, when he comes back."

Before the Philippines fell to the Japanese, someone sent my father a picture of Jack standing at attention with some other men at the edge of a clearing. He was wearing khakis and a helmet, and had a gun hanging from his shoulder. Another illustrated article from an army dispatch showed three captains named Clark in the Marine contingent on Corregidor, sitting at what looked like a picnic table. As soon as these items arrived, my father put them on the front page of the paper to keep the readers informed on the whereabouts of "the *Post*'s publisher." Though he put his own name on the masthead, he always said that he was just pinch-hitting as editor "for the duration."

One rainy Friday night when we go to pick him up, my father is in the Bright Spot. Mother goes into the tavern, leaving us to wait in the car. We are parked in front of a small grocery store run by a Greek family. Next door to the grocer is the dingy store front of a small insurance office where a large, dusty jade plant is surrounded by dead flies. I try to count them through the car window. The convertible smells of damp canvas and leather. My brother and I play a punching game in the back seat. When I get tired of the game, I start to cry, hoping Mother will come tell him to stop. She doesn't come back for a long time. After a while, the Greek comes out and brings us each a banana.

❦

While Jack was a prisoner, Aunt Lil received cards and letters from his many friends. This made her uncomfortable. "They all sound like sympathy cards," she said. My mother said, "Time hangs heavy on her hands."

ॐ

Though we seldom turned it on, the small chandelier in our living room highlighted the richness of the cedar-beamed ceiling. One evening I'd snuck part-way down the stairs to see what was going on. The light was on. Several card tables were set up under the its rosy light, but it didn't look like it would be a bridge party. My father was arranging skinny boxes full of tall yellow envelopes next to a calculating machine. He thumbed through the fat envelopes in the boxes, selected one, pulled out papers, made notes, slid his pencil over his ear, added columns of numbers, wrote an answer. These were the records from printing jobs that had been finished and delivered. But not billed.

Uncle Jack had probably taken care of the job envelopes every week, perhaps on Monday afternoon, so that the shop's billing would be prompt (and paychecks would correspond to work done), improving the chances for a steady income for the business. Letters he sent to my father after he left indicate that he had good business sense. With plenty else to do, my father let this task slide until it became a crisis.

I realize now that figuring the cost of a printing job is a perfect real-life problem for fifth grade arithmetic. "A printer worked 1.5 hours @ $2.00/hour, the press time was 0.5 hours @ $20/hour, paper costs $.10/sheet and the job used 200 sheets, overhead is 20%. How much should we charge the customer? Check your math." But my father didn't think of this as a story problem or a game, and seemed to begrudge the time and effort involved in figuring the many jobs.

I longed to punch the keys and pull the lever of the calculating machine. I wasn't yet a fifth grader and I wasn't invited to help, so I just leaned on the cedar railing of the kids' outpost and watched until Mother sent me back to bed.

ॐ

Our lumber town spread from clearings beside the Chehalis and Wishkah Rivers, across flood plains and then gradually followed the logging operations up the slopes to dryer land on the hills. Many stately homes soon graced the large plateau at the top of Broadway. Sixth Street extended westward until it came to a halt at a deep ravine. In the bottom of the gully a small stream wound past huge burned out stumps of old growth red cedar. Marshy areas stank of skunk cabbage, tall bracken ferns filled open places, fans of white fungus sprouted out of decaying logs, and lanky second-growth alder and maple fought for the sunlight. Trails led from the stream bottom to every house above it.

In the 1920s a large wooden bridge was built to span the gully and open up the next hill for residences. My grandfather bought the first flat lot beyond the bridge and built a large house above the street. That was Uncle Jack's house now, where Aunt Lil and Johnny lived.

The house with the cedar-beamed ceiling my grandfather built for us perched above his house on a level of its own on the wooded hillside. The site was between two streets and well below the cellar of the uphill neighbor's house. It could be reached only by a steep drive descending from Seventh Street—it felt like an afterthought. A steep slippery trail wound down the hillside from our basement door to the lawn of the big house. On the side toward Grandfather's house, we had a small lawn that ended in the cliff carved out years before to allow for his driveway and garages below. Once our house was built, my parents hacked brush, dug out roots, and my father built a small retaining wall and concrete path, so we could walk down the hillside to the big house without slipping in mud. Shaded by the many hemlocks and spruces on the hillside, the pink climber roses above the wall grew gray with mildew each spring.

☙

After a family Easter breakfast of baked ham and eggs and Southern Comfort for the adults, someone took a photo of the guests. My father and his friend Bill O'Connor each hold a glass of whiskey. They are both too old or too burdened to have gone to war. The others in the group are women and children: my father's Aunt Klara, Johnny's Austrian grandmother, Fran O'Connor, and aunts from both sides of the family, including two who will be widowed by the end of the war. Several of the women are wearing hats, having just come from church. I don't know who was left to take the picture. I recall feeling quite grownup, wearing a beret above my first permanent wave. The blonde baby I was holding was my sister Kristine, who was born in May 1942, just after Doolittle's raid on Tokyo, which is how my father was tracking things. By that Easter of 1943, three uncles were overseas and one more, Alec, was getting ready to leave the shop to go to San Diego as a marine drill instructor.

☙

I have few memories of things my father said during these years. Was it because he was "a working fool" as our neighbor Fran said of him? He seldom rested when he was at home because there were so many projects— shelves and walls to be built in the laundry room, a concrete path down the hill, a new garage, concrete walls in the driveway. I may not have heard him talk, to me or anyone, but I surely felt his sadness. The house was filled with the music from his records, pieces with haunting progressions of chords in minor keys, wailing horns: *Mood Indigo*. Sometimes, *I'll never smile again*.

☙

Among the things I brought home after my mother died is the soft suede pouch that Mother had said was one of my father's wallets. It is large enough to hold business-size letters, and bears the statement: "Compliments of Hayes & Hayes Bankers, Aberdeen, Washington." Though the tan suede seems good as new, that bank closed in 1927 due to the chicanery of its owner, Billy Patterson. The pouch is stuffed with papers. I would guess that my father inherited it partially filled when *his* father died and just added to it. I've looked at some of the contents already: a telegram from Kearny sent September 30, 1925 from Newark; a copy of the settlement of his mother's estate in 1929; the telegram to his father announcing his marriage to Dorothy Nielsen in March 1930. In addition, there are holy cards from nuns who admired J.W.; the receipt for a payment on account to Swedish Hospital in Seattle the month before J.W. Clark Sr. died there; a clipping of J.W.'s editorial eulogizing his eldest, Perry Clark. Among the old photos, two are noteworthy: a pre-teen Kearny with tall brother Perry, who is wearing a jaunty cap and high school letter sweater, and another on another day, with Jack in striped shirt and tie, young Kearny peering out from between his legs. Kearny looks pleased in each photo to be rubbing elbows (or knees) with the admired older brother. He lost the shelter of both of them by the time he was thirty-three.

☙

A woman's scream comes from down the hillside. I jump out of the plum tree where I've been shaking raindrops off the leaves. Baby Kris watches me from inside a circle of low edging fence stuck in the lawn. Mother empties out her apron full of green beans from our part of the neighborhood Victory Garden. She's been getting the beans ready to cook: cut and pull the string, snap the bean into pieces, then drop into a pan: snap, snap, pong, pong, pong. Snap, snap...A wail follows the scream. As we run down the path we see what's wrong. Cousin Johnny is trying to drag his grandmother away from something scary. A large green banana slug inches slowly across the walkway, waving its antennae and leaving a shiny trail that Johnny won't cross. It isn't clear who is more frightened, the four-year-old or the old lady. Carefully avoiding the slime, my mother picks up the child and carries him up to the lawn and returns to the green beans. Snap, snap, pong...

She said later she thought that grandmother was giving Johnny all kinds of fears. "What he needs is his father."

Another afternoon we were having tea at Aunt Lil's. This had been my grandfather's house, with the library lined with books to the ceiling, the thick patterned rug, and a grand piano in the living room. After setting the tray with the teapot and cups on the coffee table, Aunt Lil showed us the package she was assembling to give to the Red Cross, who promised to somehow get it to the prison camp. In early 1944, after almost two years of silence, two years of not knowing whether he was still alive, she had received several censored postcards from Jack.

The package wasn't very big. It held some canned food, cigarettes, and a deck of cards. She had cut open the deck to insert trimmed photos of herself and Johnny, and carefully resealed the cellophane. Johnny looked funny these days, because he had to wear a black patch over one eye to cure something called "lazy eye." He usually wore a white shirt and blue wool short pants with suspenders, but with the eye patch he looked like a small pirate. He wasn't wearing the patch in the picture she put in the deck. Uncle Jack used to play the piano, but I wondered if he liked to play cards.

❦

Even my Girl Scout troop joined the war effort. We hounded our neighbors for tinfoil, fat, and metal. My friend Joanne got her father to drive us up and down every street in "Finn Town," where people drank a lot of coffee, asking for newspapers and coffee jars. We didn't have to pay for the gasoline, and we thought we were helping win the war.

When we heard that the government needed rubber, I searched our house and found only an old hot water bottle, a torn bathing cap, and some rubber toys. Not worth bothering with.

But one day the weather was good after school and I went to play in the gully where friends and I spent a lot of time in the creek—we called it The Crick. We would look for periwinkles and wedge boards into the sandy bottom to create lakes and waterfalls. After a while I headed home, taking a path I seldom used, going up toward my uncle's house. I encountered a hillside covered with leaves, but it also seemed soft and a little bouncy. I stumbled over an old tire and fell into a pile of lawn trimmings. The dank smell of rotting grass was overwhelming. But instead of shaking off, I kicked around on the slope and found another tire. Rubber! I ran home to tell my mother and ask for help. Those were my aunt's yard clippings but I was afraid to ask her.

Mother easily persuaded Aunt Lil—rubber would help the war effort. Lil thought there might be an old hose in the grass pile, too. Over the next few days my Girl Scout friends and I pulled, hauled and dragged muddy tires and yard after yard of old red and green garden hose up out of the hillside, snaking it through my aunt's always tidy yard and into Bill O'Connor's wood truck. Mud and decaying grass stuck to the hoses and smeared all over Aunt Lil's walks and pavement.

After I hosed off her lawn and driveway, Lil gave me a hug. "You're a good kid, Miss Klara Nancy."

ॐ

The last of the studio portraits taken of my father was for high school graduation in 1925, when he was going on seventeen. The smooth-faced young man barely smiling above a bow tie and starched white collar is not the father I remember. His hair is brushed into a smooth curl above his forehead. My father was older and never had enough hair to show any curl. We don't have many pictures of him.

There was a movie star in *Casablanca* who always reminded me of my father. Mostly the actor played a sinister foreigner, but I knew better. He had a gentle smile, even when he was being evil. Peter Lorre. He had a large forehead, a nice face, and I always noticed his eyes: heavy lidded, there was something familiar about them. I was sure he was bashful. In some roles he wore the same rumpled hat my father wore. He was the same age as my father and had his own problems with illness and addiction. Born a Jew in what is now Slovakia, he got into the movies in Germany and Austria, but came to Hollywood before Hitler annexed Austria. When he played Mr. Moto, a Japanese detective, he even wore my father's wire-rimmed glasses. Lorre later suffered a massive, and fatal, stroke, as would my father.

☙

A yellowed headline was taped to the wall beside a grimy Mexican pot on the ledge above our dining room doorway. In the doorjamb, carved names and dates proved I would never be as tall as my brother. A pot of meat and potatoes simmered on the stove. Dinner waited until my father got home and was ready to go to the dining room.

Mother got out ice cubes and poured jiggers of rum into painted glasses and filled them with Coca Cola. At our house Coke was for the adults. She passed one glass to my father, who sat at the kitchen table staring angrily at the newspaper. She returned to her perch on the stool and set her drink on the counter. Part of the paper was spread out on the extended breadboard in front of her.

H.V. Kaltenborn's voice booming from the radio scared baby Kris. My father wouldn't talk until he'd had a second drink, and then he began.

"They won't make it. They waited too long." The familiar lament. When my father talked about Roosevelt, he made fun of the way the president talked: "I hate war, my wife Eleanor hates war, my dog Fala hates war." "Wah-er" is how Daddy said it. He ranted about how the President sent Eleanor to review the Pacific troops, which had, he was sure, delayed the invasion of the Philippines.

My father read accounts in three newspapers about the Philippine campaign. He published any news of Jack sent by the Marine Corps public relations office or from the postcards sent through the Red Cross: "Harbor *Post* Publisher Writes from Prison," for example. Jack's last, long, letter was written from Bilibid prisoner of war camp in Manila as American planes attacked the island for the first time in two and one-half years. He said he was in "the final draft of able-bodied prisoners to be shipped to Japan." The letter was found when the camp was liberated, but Jack was no longer there. My father printed the whole letter in a nice pamphlet to give to all Jack's friends.

And we waited.

When the telegram came in July of 1945 there was no more rankling over rum and Coca Cola. We heard nothing more about the Philippine campaign or MacArthur. Mother took down the headline and washed the Mexican pot. The crumpled three-year-old clipping in the garbage quoted General MacArthur: "I came out of Bataan and I shall return."

৺

My father didn't go to many movies. Once home, that's where he wanted to stay. When he agreed to an outing, we didn't leave the house until he was ready. The ushers flashed a little light to lead us to seats. We'd sit through whatever was on the screen, and the newsreels, and the second feature, and back to the first. I was mesmerized by the glamour on what the newsreels called "the silver screen." Eventually Mother would say, "This is where we came in," and we got up to leave, even though I was still trying to piece together the threads of the main feature. I don't think I ever saw a first-run movie from the beginning until I went away to college. My father may not have identified himself with Peter Lorre, but I'll bet he enjoyed the movies Lorre made with Sydney Greenstreet, *The Maltese Falcon*, for one.

My father didn't have that deep voice or foreign accent, but he did enjoy affecting a Russian accent once in a while, "Rah-sha vants nuss-ing from the YOU-nighted States," —during the Stalin years— or the mock German we learned from the Katzenjammer Kids comic strip—"Vots viss der President?" Or he would look at you as he knocked the tobacco out of his pipe, wiggle his ears, and say, "Nov shmoz ka pop."

৺

In August Mother took us children for a vacation at Hood's Canal, an arm of Puget Sound. While my father stayed behind to work, we stretched out on the wooden dock, swam in the warm salty water and poked around in shell-littered pools at low tide. Leaving the canal heading east, we soon drove onto a high dock in Bremerton to wait for a ferry to Seattle. I was fidgeting, kicking the spongy wood of the dock's pilings, feeling a cool mist on my legs as it sprayed back, looking down at clusters of purple mussels, bands of barnacles. Suddenly we heard horns honking, and whistles, and a church bell. This was it. Some sailors on the approaching ferry threw their caps in the air and shouted, "Hooray!" "We won!" We had beaten "the Japs." I thought this must be the most wonderful, happy moment that we'd waited for all these years. It was all over now. I was surprised to see my mother, who never cried, in tears.

৺

Mother often retold the story of the emotional leave-taking by the local Marines at our Northern Pacific train station at the foot of Broadway, the last time most of us saw Jack. During the war years my father drove downtown with little Kristine many evenings in time to see the arrival of the evening train. I picture them standing hand in hand beside the tracks, feeling the breeze as the train drew into the station. They could see the steam and shudder at the whistle, feel the pounding of the rolling wheels in their feet. When the sounds ebbed, they could watch the men unload the evening mail. For Kristine it was an exciting outing. For my father, what? I know he loved the wistful sound of train whistles, the excitement of an approaching train, the restlessness of the switch engine. Perhaps he hoped that one day when the train stopped, his brother would step onto the platform and cease to be The Man Who Wasn't There.

Instead, on that much-dreaded day in July 1945, with the telegram on the desk, my father sat at his green Corona portable in what he thought of as his brother's office and wrote an open letter to Jack's son and an obituary for his brother.

He expressed the hope that Johnny, who was six years old, would not mind his publishing this letter because he knew many "other folks...who have kept the torch lighted" for Jack's return would want to read it.

"It all happened six months ago," he wrote. American forces had not yet landed on Luzon, but they had bombed numbers of unmarked ships leaving Manila Harbor. "The ship on which [Capt. Clark] was being removed from the Philippines to Japan was sunk," the Marine commandant reported. My father and Aunt Lil had letters from some surviving Marines who reported that Jack survived one such bombing, but was immediately put on another ship. Either that went down, as the officials thought, or he died at sea before the ship reached Japan, but in any case my father now had the official word that his brother "had lost his life at sea."

My father had worse to tell Johnny. "A young navy flier who used to work in Jack's print shop was on this [bombing] strike [in December] and...described to me the way they worked on any Jap troopship. He held little hope for any who might be aboard." It must have been hard for my father to describe this episode.

In the eulogy for his brother my father wrote that "the first swearing [Jack] learned was in Polish" from the kids who played on the West End playground near their first home. He recounted details of Jack's life prior to going on active duty, his years at Stanford, his management of the business, his active role in the "promotion of civic affairs [which] won not only a number of very fine friends from all walks of life but picked up [for him] a few malignant enemies." Kearny noted that those enemies were guilty of "advertising extensively" that Jack was one of ten suspects in the unsolved and widely publicized murder of Laura Law in early 1940, and said for the record, that "whoever made this charge are liars." (The family speculated that Jack was targeted as a suspect because he was a prominent businessman and the victim was the pretty young wife of a radical union leader.)

The reluctant new publisher of the *Post* laid out his long letter to his nephew and the obituary on the front page below the image of the telegram that covered part of the nameplate —the week's news could wait. He ended by telling Johnny,

> Your dad was a mighty fine husband, brother and friend...and a mighty fine father too\....He owes none of us anything. Maybe that is what the Marine Corps commander means when he tells us that Jack is now, 'Carried on the rolls of the Marine Corps as having been killed in action in the performance of his duty and service of his country.' That's like saying the account has been paid in full. That is something for you to be proud of.

He signed the letter K. Clark.

My father's papers contained the poem "Away" by James Whitcomb Riley. Typed on a half sheet of newsprint, the poem was worn and stained from having been stowed in his wallet. It had been included in the editorial column of the *Post* when J.W. died in 1935. My father had been carrying it a long time. The first and last stanzas of the poem:

> *"I cannot say, and I will not say*
> *That he is dead— He is just away!*
> ...
> *"Think of him still as the same, I say:*
> *He is not dead—he is just away."*

Pressroom after the first fire at Quick Print Co., 1948

The end of the story: scrapping the type

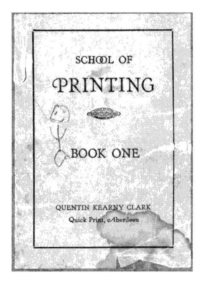

SCHOOL OF

PRINTING

BOOK ONE

QUENTIN KEARNY CLARK
Quick Print, Aberdeen

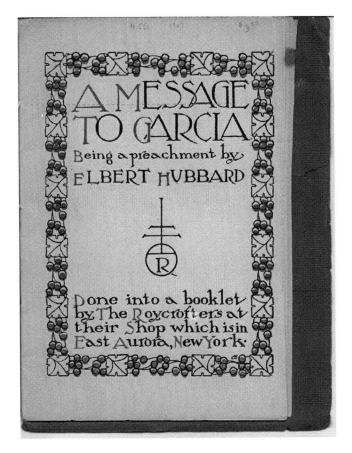

1899 pamphlet from the library of J.W. Clark

One Man's Happy Family

*It must be admitted that too large a proportion of married women do not find
in marriage that quietude and satisfaction which they have been led to expect.*
— J. H. Kellogg, M.D., *Man the Masterpiece*, 1907

"[As] I am writing to you, I am confronted with the loss of my brother, Jack,"
my father wrote on 23 July, 1945 in a letter accompanying a one-page will.
Having just composed the obituary for his brother, he must have thought it
time to face his own demise. My father declared his desire that "all such
worldly possessions as are rightfully considered mine so to do with,...shall,...
become the worldly possessions of my very dear wife, Dorothy." The longest
paragraph of the will recalled and dealt with a debt of $100.00 owed to his
son, a sum given to Phil some ten years earlier by J.W. Clark.

My father addressed the letter to Mother and to his (then) three
children, asking us to "work with Lillian and Johnny," Jack's widow and
son, in straightening out the intertwining of the Clark brothers' affairs,
many the result of their father's will.

He wrote, "My dad used to drive it through our heads that the 'Clarks
stuck together...' and my dad used to tell us to 'do the right thing...do the
best you can.'" As Mother told us and as I well knew, my father tried to live
up to his father's expectations every day of his life. He could not ignore the
overarching legacy of The Boss. He could not forget him.

To us, Phil, Kristine (Kristy at that time), and me, my father wrote:
"You've been the source of a tremendous lot of pleasure and pride through
the years that we have lived together. Our home has been a real one, worthy
of everything that such a name ever implied." He urged us to "be considerate
of your mama. She will see that she holds up her end of the deal." He referred
to his "mistakes," without listing any, but "I cannot ask for forgiveness, and
I really do not want any. Like Popeye used to say, 'I yam what I yam and
that's all that I yam.'"

🙟

I'm touched by the letter, by its humility, but also mystified by it. He described an idyllic family. He made us sound like Dick and Jane, Sally and Spot, the Mother and Father, the perfect people in a tidy house on a tidy street with sidewalks, whom I met in my first-grade readers.

We might have looked like that kind of family to the outside world. My father went to work every day, though not in a business suit. My mother wore housedresses, did the wash on Monday, the ironing on Tuesday, if it hadn't rained. She dressed up and went to teas and raised money for the Seattle Children's Orthopedic Hospital. On Sunday she took us to church while our father read the paper at home. We sat together at the dinner table, though sometimes the meat had dried out and the gravy congealed because we'd waited a long time for Daddy to get home.

But my father seldom took part in those dinner table conversations. He was silent, mum's the word, as if he'd taken to heart the advice on propaganda posters showing a stern Uncle Sam signaling: *Loose lips sink ships, Careless talk gets there first...*

Almost like a stage director, Mother carried the talk around the dinner table. She'd draw each of us out, respond with things my father should have said, and tell stories about each of us—Phil's sports and trombone lessons, my Girl Scouts, Kristy's latest achievements. In this memory, one-and-a-half-year-old Kristy loved to play in the dirt, loved to watch the dogs and the birds.

Viewed from afar we were a perfect family. But I remember not being able to sleep, and grinding my teeth and having tense dreams when I did sleep. I remember endlessly waiting in the car outside the Bright Spot. I remember listening for my father's car to come down the driveway. Anxieties I only later came to understand.

᠅

In the winter of 1946 many deliveries disturbed the order in our house. A cabinetmaker installed wall-hung bookshelves in the room we still called the nursery, just off the kitchen, the room converted from a one-car garage to be a bedroom when Kristine joined the family in 1942. It would again become a nursery when Mother came home with Kathy the summer of 1949. But this fall it was to become a library. Aunt Lil and young Johnny were moving into an apartment. Bit by bit our share of my grandfather's treasures came in the door.

The sturdy oak furniture seemed out of scale for our modest house, but Grandpa Clark had bought it, it bore the Roycroft symbol and the deeply-incised family name. We would fit it in. I enjoyed helping move the books into the new shelves. Many of them had been printed by the Roycrofters of East Aurora, New York. I felt like a librarian as I organized the leather-bound books and started typing catalog cards to put in a wooden file drawer that also arrived, one of many tasks I began but did not finish in those years.

One day I tried to get comfortable in the big Morris chair with one of Elbert Hubbard's *Little Journeys*, a volume describing his visits to homes of famous artists. I hoped to find information for a book report about one of them. The soft tooled-leather binding felt good to the touch and I liked turning the thick textured paper with untrimmed edges. The dramatic page layouts and clearly printed lettering were admirable. But the text! Boring. An unsophisticated reader then, I didn't analyze the writing style. I now might describe it as egocentric impressionist. Hubbard thought highly of his own opinions. I took this as a lesson: make sure the contents are worthy before you pretty up the container—a hard one for a printer who is asked to produce quality product but not often allowed to choose the text.

Hubbard today is remembered mostly for his aphorisms, which appear regularly in the Cryptoquote puzzles in my local newspaper. Of his writings, only the strange preachment, "A Message to Garcia" earns much recognition. My fragile 1899 Roycroft imprint of that relic of "this Cuba business" may be a collector's item.

❦

Along with the books came a tall figurine, the manly, stern-faced Napoleon, arms folded high on his chest, booted legs in full step, suggesting at once refinement, commanding authority and a sense of foreboding. I believe my grandfather had this same effect on his family, on my father. This avatar now commands attention on a ledge in my dining room.

If any of us had thought of forgetting old J.W., it would be harder than ever. His Morris chairs, his library table with the Tiffany-style stained glass lamp, handsome books, and large dictionary now filled our tiny library, née nursery née garage. The round fumed-oak dining table, sideboard and many chairs, also sturdy Roycroft items, filled the ten-by-ten dining room to bursting. Mother had a low table made of two of the table's extension boards, which eventually provided a place for the family's first television set.

I don't know how my father felt about being surrounded by his family's furnishings. He worked long hours in the print shop set up by his father and brother, and now came home to rooms-full of their things as well. The ballast of the Old Man's life became a burden that weighed down his life, and yet it gave character and stability to my growing up and formed the great conundrum that I had to unravel in order to understand my father's life, and its impact on my own.

I never learned to call J.W. "Grandpa" because he died when I was two, but I always felt that he must have dandled me on his knee, as snapshots show he often held my father as an infant. I felt that I had known him and that he expected something from me and it fell to me to represent him in the world. It was he who gave infant me the boyish nickname that my father rejected, and that I happily embraced as I went off to college. We felt his absence from our lives as surely as we felt the presence of his expectations.

ᘐ

My thoughts ramble from room to room tracing the patrimonial insertions into my childhood home. The large clock with its bookcase found space outside my bedroom door and would faithfully chime ever quarter hour if someone remembered to wind it. Treasures nestled into every nook and cranny, except for the kitchen, but my recollections settle in the kitchen with its percolator still warm on the stove and a relentless view of alder trees. One kitchen memory still generates shivers: My father has cut down several gangly hemlock trees on the hillside below the house, and begins clearing out the limbs and remaining roots and brush with a peavey. Somehow it spears his calf. I'll always remembered that strange logger's tool and its ugly name because of what I see in the kitchen. He stands quietly with his foot on a chair, pants leg pulled up above his knee, blood seeping down the calf and soaking into his stocking. Mother probes the wound with the long glass dauber covered with tincture of iodine. I know how that must feel and cringe every time she draws the wand from the bottle, the dreaded rusty liquid dripping on everything. I'm sorry to think that he'll have to suffer again as she probes the gash. He doesn't say a word as she stanches the wound and bandages it. Later I understand that I have an image to go with the word *stoic.*

ᘐ

Our kitchen not only doubled as an emergency room, it operated as a bustling train station, with exits to the library/nursery, the dining room and to the tiny hall that opened to the basement, a half-bath, and the front hallway. Baskets of laundry freighted through from the basement to the mangle and ironing board in the nursery. The grocery boy hefted our order from the front door to the counter. Big collie dogs shuttled back and forth or sprawled in the center. Muddy children scurried through to the bathroom. The stove, sink, and refrigerator lined the walls to support the station's short-order diner, as Mother joked, and a small round table stood in everybody's way.

In comparison, the equally small dining room, with only two doorways, provided a calm siding—everything that needed a flat surface parked there. Sewing projects or gift wrapping took over the table. When a new baby arrived in the house—during the war, Kristine, then several new cousins—the layette took over the table to receive the dripping infant from the kitchen sink, there to be dried, oiled, and cuddled. In high school I closed the kitchen's swinging door to have a quiet place to finish my shorthand homework before dinner, because I had a club meeting in the evening.

One winter after the war, Mother spread books and ledger sheets on the table—by then it was the sturdy round oak table—to do *her* homework. She had enrolled in an evening bookkeeping class at the junior college and enjoyed learning a new skill. The careful rows of legible numbers entered on pages with many columns and many-colored rulings looked interesting, my first glimpse of double-entry bookkeeping. Both of my sisters mastered the subject years later.

My father didn't mind that Mother might take a night out after dinner on Mondays to go to a movie, any movie, with her friend Fran O'Connor. But he minded greatly her going out for what she claimed was a class at the college. She didn't get to finish the course. Though I only later heard Mother's account of his reasoning, he accused her of going out to find another man. For a businessman who couldn't keep up with his paperwork, scolding his wife for trying to learn a useful skill didn't make sense. But then, jealousy is never rational.

☙

The print shop suffered a fire just after I entered my sophomore year in high school. I'd spent time after school that fall learning to number ballots. The fire broke out on a Thursday evening in September after closing hours. One side of the paper was ready to roll, loaded up with ads for candidates in the coming primary election. Flyers promoting candidates sat on the wrapping table ready to be delivered. I'd overheard sarcastic comments in the back shop about the candidate for Sheriff whose handout showed him wearing a white Stetson. Most of the county's primary ballots had been numbered and wrapped, the Poll Books had been delivered. The Aberdeen Fire Department got the call, "come to 127 South G Street, upstairs," from the telephone switchboard in Anchorage, Alaska.

My father's high school friend John Forbes, who wrote the news and solicited ads for the *Post*, had come in late that September evening to finish his work and to talk on the phone with the woman he was courting, then living in Alaska. A round-faced, jovial man with a fine radio voice, John had a passion for steelhead fishing. From his desk in the "Hell Hole" beside the bindery room, he saw flames flash into the back of the stock room beyond. Apparently the long distance operator heard him say to the woman, "My God, the shop's on fire." The Anchorage operator said, "Where are you? Give me the address," and made the call to the fire station three blocks away from the shop. That was September 9, 1948. Several days later an article appeared in Italics in the center of the front page of the delayed *Post*,

> *Due to conditions*
> *beyond our control - - -*
> *your Grays Harbor Post is somewhat late this week.*
> *It is considerably earlier, however, than was thought possible early Friday morning as the staff prowled through the debris that only a fire can leave.*
> *A chain of circumstances adds up to one sum ... luck.*
> *In the first place someone was in the plant when the fire broke out; secondly the fire department had a short run when time was vital; in the third place, while there was considerable damage, none to equipment was irreparable, and after a day of digging out it is a pleasure to say that practically everything works....*

Photographs taken that Friday morning, presumably for insurance purposes, show that the fire started behind the big press where the long inky rollers lined up beside the sink, and flashed up into the corner next to the stock room. Only two closed windows and the backs of storage shelves separated the press room from the stock room. Remarkably little had caught fire in this room full of paper.

My father acknowledged the lateness of the paper and the fire in a few brief paragraphs in the editorial section. He thanked the fire chief and his men for efficient action to stop a blaze that, "due to the construction of the building, might have spread through an entire section of the block...." A long hallway connected the print shop's space above the plumbing business to the paint shop around the corner on Market Street. "We are grateful for the offers of help received from Harbor printers and from representatives of Puget Sound suppliers. To everyone we say thanks for lending a helping hand.

"When the old meal ticket gets all cleaned up and going next week we hope to be back on schedule as usual."

❦

At home life must have gone on seamlessly in spite of the fire. What I remember of that fall was being in the same Advanced Algebra class with my brother, which he hated.

In fact, life returned to such a state of dailiness, that, in spite of Mother's basal metabolism temperature charts, which I'd seen when snooping in her dresser drawer but didn't understand until my own marriage, she conceived again about a month after the fire. This led to the colorful scene involving the almost adult son and his pregnant mother and abashed father. Mother stayed close to home that spring, letting me, still too young to have a driver's license, take the wheel to run her errands. Kristine was seven and I was almost sixteen when our caboose, Kathy, arrived the summer after the fire.

I can only speculate on whether jealousy or that shop fire kindled the unexpected embers in the parental marriage bed. In any case, Kathy became the freshly bathed and cooing baby taking over the dining table mornings, who kept Mother's energy and attention firmly centered at home for some years. In an aspiring middle-class family like ours, my father had bought further into the Dick-and-Jane-family ideal in the years when Rosie the Riveter was supposed to return to the kitchen, and business was a man's world. Never mind that his bright wife would willingly help. Never mind that he needed help.

My father's optimistic spin on adversity carried the day. The business would survive, he would continue to comment on the passing scene in his editorials, at least for now. We were unaware that a mental breakdown loomed on the horizon.

❦

After his death, Mother canonized my father. When a few drinks loosened her lips, she talked about having been married to a wonderful man, a great husband. She believed in that perfect family and insisted on keeping the myth alive. I doubted the accuracy, or sincerity, of her assertions when in the 1970s she admitted that a particular popular song got to her: *Little Things Mean a Lot*, often sung by Kitty Kallen. The sentiment in the lyrics brought her to tears. I had seen how one-sided their relationship had been; she had to reach out for *his* hand, she had to tell him he looked nice when he cleaned up, she offered him reassurance.

Wrapped up in his own troubles, my father didn't fuss over birthdays or anniversaries, and he didn't observe humdrum conventions such as inquiring about her day. Though taciturn to the core, give him a whee'barra and a beer, a shovel, and some boards, and he produced a fine product. He took on the big things, like building forms for a retaining wall, painstakingly threading in reinforcing rods to make it strong before shoveling in the hand-mixed concrete. After dinner he settled into his chair in the corner. Who could begrudge him his pipe, his music—the usual strains of *Melancholy Baby*. At least he was home. We were all Clarks living together in the house my grandfather built, a convincing picture of a happy, trouble-free family, convincing, perhaps, even to us.

MAY ASK LEAGUE TO GUARD POLAND

Lacarno Delegates Believe That France Will Accept Compromise

SECURITY ACCORD NEAR?

Czechoslavakia Willing to Exchange Egis of Paris for That of Geneva if France Can Obtain Guaranties.

LOCARNO, Switzerland, October 14 (A. P.)—If France can obtain suitable guaranties for her eastern allies it seems probable that she

Fig. 10—Four-deck newspaper head showing (A) the dropline, (B) inverted pyramid, (C) crossline, (D) hanging indention, and (E) jim dash.

Headline examples from a Printing Lesson

The Editor's Legacy

As a cub at this business of expressing an opinion, this writer takes an 'I'm from Missouri' [The Show Me state] attitude toward the 'third' New Deal.
— Kearny Clark, editorial, 1941

Not everyone gets to carry home a nine-pound book the size of a newspaper broadsheet. I felt lucky to own such a volume, but no one envied me as I struggled onto the airport bus with the book, a purse, and a rolling suitcase. It was the 1990s and I had been visiting Kristine and doing research in the Hoover archives at Stanford for my next project. But for its size, with its blue cloth binding and printed spine, the book looked like any other hardcover tome. A man seated across from me made a joke about it being "serious reading matter." I felt a little silly. Trying to keep the thing out of people's way, it came close to my face and the smell of mildew was unmistakable.

And was even stronger when I opened a volume. Years later, in spite of being sheltered in a dry Salt Lake City closet, these huge books still exuded must, the familiar, suffocating odor of my childhood sleeping bag.

Eventually I brought home the thirteen volumes of the *Grays Harbor Post* that had been kept in one dingy storage unit or another after my mother moved out of our house. My parents had saved copies of the 1940 decade because those years' issues contained "The Kitchen Critic" column written by their friend Kathy Hogan, who was a talented observer and storyteller. At one time my father took the set to Kathy so that she could "do something" with her columns, such as pull them together into a book. She fussed over the volumes a bit, put in some colored book marks, made lists of themes—during the war she had written about the National Guard soldiers guarding the beach, victory gardens, beachcombing, and eccentric neighbors—and left a few notes in them. One note scrawled on the back of an envelope was a long list of symptoms she must have planned to take to her doctor—though clearly not well, she lived another decade. Without the copy machines, character recognition scanners, and computers that became available later, she had no idea how to proceed. Soon enough, she demanded that my mother take back the volumes. Kathy had feared her house at the beach, far from any fire department, would burn to the ground as her neighbor's had that year, and they would be lost. After I brought the books home, my friend Lucy Hart and I took on the project, and published *Cohassett Beach Chronicles: World War II in the Pacific Northwest* by Kathy Hogan in 1995, twenty-two years after her death.

These volumes of the *Post* were one of the greatest gifts my parents could have given me. Kathy Hogan's writings coincided with my Aberdeen school years, from 1939 to 1951. The paper had recorded the comings and goings of my town, my family, and my young life. There it was, a personal, if cumbersome, diary.

Once they are lined up in the guest closet, I can leaf through them at my leisure, though they are awkward to read. My favorite reading stand is the creamy baby grand piano in the sunroom. As I stand in the graceful curve of the piano case I recall a time as a girl when Mother and I used the *Post*'s free tickets to attend a Community Concert. A substantial and elegantly gowned soprano stood in the curve of a Steinway piano holding a lacy handkerchief and sang endless German Lieder. But now I am not standing there to sing. Rather, I face the piano and the big book propped open on its lid, my legal pad and pen ready, and start reading a year in the life of our small lumber town at the confluence of the Chehalis and Wishkah Rivers, a year in my life. If I pay attention, I'll find the article telling who was the ponderous soprano, and whose lieder she sang.

To rest my eyes from time to time, I look out the window. Traffic whizzes up the hill beyond our row of pine trees, and because I am in close contact with the piano, I sometimes take a break to play a simple sonatina.

❧

I am drawn to the pages of the *Post* and my father's editorials like an inexperienced beekeeper seeking honey. I hope to be rewarded with some nugget, a honeycomb of family happenings, forgotten gossip and news, but am leery of encountering stinging opinions and political views that I'll find disappointing. My father liked what he read in the three conservative papers that came into the house daily, and he probably voted for Republicans. He was a self-taught writer. As editor, he was expected to write up to twenty-two column inches of "enlightened" opinion every week. He developed a style and occasionally used colorful language. He scorned the kind of "highfaluting tributes" others might write. His sarcasm and the way he sniffed out hypocrisy, a skill he may have inherited from his father, is wonderfully refreshing. To generate the weekly epistle, he would find a hook, a metaphor, or a device around which to build an argument favoring or mocking some public policy or person or event.

He was critical of international summits that occurred near the end of World War II, when Roosevelt, and later Truman, were too easily, he felt, hoodwinked by Russia's Joseph Stalin. In August 1948 he wrote about the Danube Conference: "Old Joe and his bevy of revamped Volga boatmen are doing a pretty fancy job of diplomatic footwork in the Old World striped-pants and swallow-tail coated business." Anticipating that Dewey would win the 1948 election, he predicted "a new broom" would sweep the "Roosevelt regime" out of Washington, and, a week later, complained that Dewey deserved to lose because he "had toned [down] his speeches to perfect generalities."

My father's understanding of national affairs does not seem dated. He wrote about a do-nothing congress, the largest budget proposal ever seen (Truman's $80 billion), free trade agreements that hurt Americans (in his world, loggers and crab fishermen). He disagreed with one of the perennial name-callers who tarred Washington as "a socialist state." He fed the local disgust with the National Park Service and the president because Olympic National Park was enlarged to take in the Hoh corridor and the coastal strip, contending that they were locking up marketable timber and making no plans to develop the new holdings.

Each Labor Day he reprinted his father's 1906 essay, "Men of the Mist," an eloquent tribute to unheralded sawmill workers. For my father it was one less editorial to write but it was also one more acknowledgment that he was living in the Old Man's shadow.

Some of his editorials brought back family scenes. In June 1950 he claimed to be "starry-eyed" about the Milky Way, which "shows to especially fine advantage in the eastern horizon on June nights." He made us all go out in the dark and look eastward. That was a first sighting for me, even though I had often slept out in our yard or on the garage roof on summer nights, a sighting I recalled with him years later in the Utah desert.

One week he apologized for the late delivery of the paper "due to on and off power...The metal used to make type is slower to heat than potatoes...." I remember that snowy winter well. Kathy was a baby and we needed to heat her bottle on the on-again off-again electric stove. Mother demonstrated a paraffin cooker in the fireplace, and there was a day when I was left in charge of the two girls while my parents drove off in a blizzard to take Phil to the plane in Seattle. My best memories of that winter include getting to wear ski pants to high school, then school being closed, and skiing on the golf course with friends, but my father wrote about broken water mains and threats to move Boeing from Seattle to Kansas for national security reasons.

In April 1949 he celebrated forty-five years of continuous weekly publication of the *Post* from the same printing plant. The front page story recalled some of the Harbor stories that his father had documented through the years, and boasted that the paper, "printed on book paper, [is] an operation that has aroused considerable awe as far away as Aberdeen, Scotland." How did he know that, I wondered, until I noticed at the bottom of the page a story quoting the letter he had received from the editor of Auld Aberdeen's *People's Journal*.

A charming photo of a litter of collie puppies also appeared on page one of that issue. Our MacDuff was the sire; I recalled that his certified papers were part of Mother's archive, so I searched out his pedigree, a family tree of fancy names and proof of the inbreeding that ensured those elegant long noses and tawny coats with perfect white neck-ruffs.

In another editorial, my father contrasted Nelson Rockefeller's observance of National Brotherhood Week with the behavior of communist rulers of Russia who were cracking down on the Catholic Church in Hungary. He urged newly re-inaugurated President Truman, faced with a recalcitrant House and filibustering Senate, to take a more conciliatory attitude toward Congress: "One catches more flies with molasses, Mr. President, than one does with vinegar." He gave his readers a vocabulary lesson after the magnitude eight earthquake one noon in April: "Granting that during a quake no one would argue the fine points of spelling out perfectly what was taking place...the Northwest is now up to the big leagues as quakes go and should be up on the right term, *temblor*." I was in study hall at the high school that noon eating a peanut butter and jelly sandwich when I saw the long bookcase in the center of the room make a snake-like maneuver before settling down. I was glad we were fifty miles from the epicenter and suffered little damage from that *temblor*.

He followed every twist in the decade-long search for oil or gas on the north coast of the Harbor, bought stock in one of the drilling companies, and took the little girls out to see one of its wells. He printed a full-page photo of a drill rig in a clearing surrounded by beach pines and gave front page coverage to optimistic claims by the drillers. Neither his nor any other well came in.

As he mocked Secretary of State Dean Acheson's prediction: "New Peace Era Ahead" which was made only days before the North Koreans crossed the 38th parallel and started the Korean Conflict, the Society Page noted that our family was vacationing at Cohassett Beach; Mother found rentals for us there over ten summers, several of those in the years after my father became sick.

Humor as well as irony and sarcasm made it into his editorials. One week he expressed satisfaction that a five-line bit of filler below a column of football scores a few weeks before had attracted some notice and appreciation. Boilerplate, he noted, was "a realm seldom mentioned except in trade circles and then only in whispers around the unwashed."[11] The item deserved comment, as it presented this little-known fact: "Eighty-five thousand frogs died last year of hernia. By proper medical care nearly 65,431 frogs ranging from three weeks to one month of age, would be alive today...." Boilerplate needed no attribution, but this sounds like something conjured up by Uncle Alec's teasing brain.

In April 1949 my father talked about the change in the "look" of the paper because he had purchased a "new series of body-types designed for easier reading.... Though smaller, it is more readable," he wrote. I wish he had included the name of the font, but in comparison with earlier issues, these pages did seem easier to read.

ॐ

The number of errors and typos I observed in my father's editorials reminded me that he often wrote them at the last minute. With the pressure of a deadline, no one read proof. The many homonyms would have been easy to miss, and they often survive today's spell checkers. For example, my wordprocessor would not make a wiggly red line under "there" in "The

---

[11]   Boilerplate is journalistic material or a syndicated feature available in plate or mat form; typically cast in a stereotype machine by a printer's devil, it is ready to be inserted anywhere in a layout for a publication.

players put there best foot forward," a line that appeared in one of his editorials.

He sometimes used a construction not often seen today—after introducing a topic, he might begin the next paragraph with "But comes now the question...."

One year, to relieve the boredom of writing the annual paean for the coming County Fair, my father recalled a delicious treat at an "old strawberry festival," a bit of nostalgia from his childhood in the days before the fair was organized. Such tidbits are the closest thing to biographical notes left to us.

Life seemed to be good for our family, as evidenced in the volumes of the *Post* from the years I was in high school. For one brief shining moment, the shop was in good shape. In August 1948, while I turned fifteen and had my tonsils removed, my father welcomed his good friend John Forbes back to town. Forbes resumed writing his weekly column, but also assembled the front-page news and managed the commercial printing. Happily he had been in the shop the night of the fire. He saw to it that several of the next years' Christmas issues ran to twelve pages, the additional pages largely containing institutional ads from local businesses. A front man at last!

☙

The last of the bound volumes of the *Post* documented my departure to college at age 18. To browse the remaining years of the paper, I would have to resort to microfilm.

And *voila!* An old Dukane microfilm reader came to the rescue. Purchased from the University of Utah's surplus stores in the 1990s, it took up residence on a former dining table in our guest room. Its case was large and battered but had the sleek styling of a two-tone hardtop. Bulky as an old TV but much wider, its screen leaned drunkenly forward toward the user. The tapes I threaded into the upper blue reel were made by the Washington State Library. Library workers had cut apart the bound volumes of the *Grays Harbor Post* held by the Aberdeen Timberland Library and filmed the pages from April 1904 until January 1961 (the cut sheets remain, stored in large boxes in the Aberdeen library). I paid $12 apiece for each two-year tape of the old paper, twenty-seven reels altogether. A bargain.

The film reader was primitive compared to the newer reader-printers and film-to-digital readers now available to library users. It allowed me to read microfilm. Period. It broke down one year, and my husband spent months tracking down replacements for the critical belts that advance the film mechanisms. When he finally got them, he wrapped them in holiday paper and tucked them under the Christmas tree.

Each time I threaded a year into the reader I hoped to find something. One spring I set out to read the later years, starting with 1953, the year my father got sick. The editorials he wrote prior to the trip to New York had contained the ponderings and opinions of a man who was keeping up with world affairs. I was curious to see what he wrote about once his paranoia took over. I wondered if I would be embarrassed by a sick man's ramblings. Would I get some inkling of his pain?

ॐ

This was a big undertaking: I would have to scan through at least 3,300 pages from those last seven or so years. I couldn't resist reading most of what streamed by on the microfilm screen. In the early fifties, after I left home, my classmates and neighborhood friends were also starting their adult lives. The society page of the *Post* reported who finished college, whom they married, where they were going to live. In the account of my friend Janet's wedding, I found a detailed description of the elegant bridesmaid dress I spent a summer sewing and sweating over. The unforgiving changeable mauve taffeta and Advanced Vogue pattern caused sweet-tempered me to rue the day I learned to sew. Of the twelve bridesmaids' dresses in the wedding photo lineup, mine was the only one that hung properly, and I wore the gown only once more, decidedly overdressed at a college party in the cellar of an Aberdeen lumber baron's home.

The sight of my engagement announcement, made on the occasion of my parents' silver wedding anniversary in 1955, became more fraught as I absorbed the fact that there was no editorial in that issue. I recalled the party. My father had seemed sheepish, almost ashamed, a long shambled way from the young man in the family scrapbook in a three-piece suit who took off in his roadster to seek his fortunes, then returned to court and marry Pete twenty-five years before.

ॐ

I need not have worried about being embarrassed by my father's ramblings. There were none.

This man who had taught himself to typeset and compose words, whole pages, whole columns, who had joined the elite group of people focused on words, whose business was putting words on paper, had written no more. How could this have happened? Before the fateful road trip to New York he had devoted his life to creating and producing crisply impressed words on fine paper, but *after* that trip, this man was silent. Though the paper continued to come out weekly, there *were* no more editorials, a sting I had not expected.

༚

My father's pen had run dry. For every issue during the paper's final 7½ years, the place below the masthead where the opinions of the editor, either those of my grandfather, my uncle, or my father, had appeared for 49 years, was devoid of an editor's presence. From the day we drove away in August 1953, the editorial slot was given over to filler.

Boilerplate. Some of it came from a national distributor along with knitting patterns, house plans, and recipes. One columnist who appeared in those first two columns for a long time was a representative of the National Association of Manufacturers—syndicated boilerplate. Several correspondents who had shared the editorial page with my father over the years, supplying jokes and bromides, migrated left on page four to fill the editorial void. The master of doggerel, who ended each "poetic line" with an asterisk, still filled his slot. Items from the *Post's* morgue, in a column titled "50 Years Ago," was added to the page.

This lack of editorial presence was a shocking confirmation of how sick my father must have been. I had really expected to see some words in their proper place. I thought I would have to read pathetic pieces, meandering mumblings. Something. All these years I had assumed that he somehow kept going. That was how well Mother shielded me. That was how determined I was to look away.

My father had a nervous breakdown. He spent time in a psychiatric hospital, he hung around the house. He couldn't write. He didn't write. How could I really not have noticed? I ached for my parents. I'd known he wasn't working. One Christmas I brought Mother a nice green plaid quilted bathrobe, "just the thing for a working woman." I knew she was trying to support the family. And yet I was in denial.

My father, the editor, had gone missing.

☙

I pressed the fast rewind button and listened to the hiss of the tape and the rattle of the reels, heard the slap, slap, slap as the tape flew out of the gate and spun loosely on the reel. Dust swirled about the glass plates in the bright light, the thick lens of the reader. I closed the last, disappointing tape. Sadness swept over me. Only for the last two issues had my favorite editor written anything. I experienced the bitterness my father must have felt, the chagrin, the cursing of human frailty, that forced him into silence. That caused him to abandon his post, his *Post*.

Examples of handsome typefaces,
neat lowercase display, and graceful borders

Get Out of Jail, Pass Go...

You do know that your father was epileptic...
—Aunt Barbara de Luna, in 1994

In 1962, a year after the demise of the *Post* and just before our move from San Rafael to southern California, I arrived in Aberdeen by train with my three young children. My husband had projects to finish at his work before the move, so I thought I could be some help to my parents at home.

Mother was working as a receptionist in a doctor's office. Kathy, whom Mother called "Rosebud" and my father called "Buster," was in the eighth grade. My father had residual nerve damage in one leg and a lot of pain because of a damaged disk. He hadn't fully recovered from disk surgery. Because of his back, because of his mental state, because he no longer owned the shop, he had nothing to do.

Every day, as he wandered about the house, which I tried for two brief weeks to keep in order, he praised me, boasted about me and my young children, and spoke with awe about my husband. He seemed childlike.

I was focused on keeping my children occupied, helping as best I could, and working hardest on not seeing anything unpleasant. Mother had learned early to avoid confrontation; when her mother engaged in "fights" with the younger children—Rhoda got right down on their level, but the kids never won—Dorothy got out of the house. My self-defense was less passive, but as effective. I didn't always want to see clearly. At a horror movie I covered my eyes in the scary scenes. (Tell me when it's over.) I could sit in a crowded room among chatting people and balance my check book or create a budget for a project. I didn't want to see my father being shiftless, weak. I never thought about him getting old or wished he would die, as Kristine did. I just attacked dusty corners, did the laundry and braided my daughters' hair. I could certainly avoid noticing what my father was doing, or not doing.

But ignoring him wasn't easy. On Valentine's Day my parents took me along to a party next door. Dr. Chuck Pollock had recently moved his family into the house that stood above ours, and had befriended our family. He sympathized with my father's problems, more aware than I of their mental component. Though a general practitioner rather than a psychiatrist, Dr. Pollock gave Mother advice about treatments for my father.

His wife Luree's homemaking skills made her neighbors feel lazy— while raising a pack of kids, she baked bread, did volunteer work at the hospital, and stayed up till all hours making costumes or caramelizing walnuts. We left Kathy in charge of my children and walked up the hill to join the guests at the Pollock's home. Luree acted as master-of-ceremonies for the party, directing juvenile games, mostly ice-breakers with a Valentine theme. To start with, we were each given a bit of construction paper and told to find a piece that fit in the hand of a guest of the opposite sex. Successful couples put together, guess what, a red heart! It went on like that. I didn't know anyone in the room but my parents, and we people from the bottom of the driveway were uncomfortable.

Over dessert and punch, we tried to make conversation with the other guests. My father began to tell a rambling story. I sensed it was going to be more appropriate for the crowd in his favorite tavern than for this whole-some, sober gathering. He smiled as he talked, enjoying having an audience. He ended with a punch-line about a "buck nigger." I froze. No one spoke.

Dr. Pollock broke the silence by insisting that he and his oldest son play their violins for us, and they sawed through "Country Gardens " and "Home on the Range," painfully out of tune and out of tempo.

The next day I fretted about why I hadn't confronted my father, or at least apologized for his racist joke. Here was one more reason to reject him.

I couldn't even tell myself that he hadn't meant it, that his illness had taken over. Rather than think about it further, and forgetting that I needed to serve an early dinner, I donned rubber gloves and slathered oven cleaner over the dark porcelain innards of my mother's stove, fully committed to the foul chore. Kathy grabbed a sandwich on her way out to a babysitting job. A few days later my children and I found our seats on the train, headed south.

Three months later Mother checked my father into the state mental hospital.

℮

On that Valentine's visit, the town had looked more bedraggled that usual. Or perhaps I projected the sense of my inadequacy and of my father's failings, onto my hometown. My father had had great hopes for Aberdeen.

He'd followed all plans to improve the Harbor's deep-water channel, and even carried around a well-worn copy of outdated Port Dock planning documents. Like his father before him, he inflated every hint or rumor that a new business might come to town or that one of the mills might start up again. As economic activity expanded along Highway 99 (now I-5) from Seattle to Portland, wasn't it only a matter of time before some of that economic bounty would spill over onto the Harbor?

Instead, over the years, businesses shut their doors, mills were torn down for scrap, his best customers left. The hospital grew, as did the junior college, but the state correctional facility on the town's edge attracted only welfare-dependent families of the inmates. A shopping mall built on the south side further propelled the decline of the downtown.

ॐ

Mother knew how to keep our troubles to ourselves. My father was well thought of in spite of his decline in his last years, but that possibility didn't keep me from judging him. Unpleasant words hover in my memories of this time: forlorn, doddering, bungling. He hadn't admitted that his mind did not just echo with negative words, but with voices. One of them saying, "One bullet will do it."

ॐ

Reluctantly, I pull out the rest of the almost illegible records from his hospital file. They take me back to 1962, where I've left my father "doing time" in the state mental hospital. Valentine's Day has come and gone, and I've moved even farther from home. I am not aware until much later that Mother has checked my father into Steilacoom.

Though hard to read and heartbreaking to absorb, the records make clear that during his stay he met with psychiatrists, a neurologist, social workers, and physical and occupational therapists. All of them thought he had a mental disorder. He spent some days puttering in the hospital's print shop and in some sort of craft workshop. He later showed me a leather bracelet, and said, "You didn't know the old man had taken up leather weaving." Though he seemed proud of his handiwork, he didn't say where he'd made it.

The neurologist examined him "to consider the possibility of an organic lesion of the brain....The patient had a history of several syncopal [fainting] attacks apparently without convulsions" during the previous several years. Dr. Lightburne found my father to be a "cheerful smiling and over-complimentary man," a man who "rambles so much it was not possible to secure an adequate neurological history." Dr. Lightburne could give "no definitive opinion" concerning his syncopal attacks. He did report on the atrophied nerves in the patient's left leg and foot from the ruptured disk, and on his "smiling inappropriate affect."

ꝫ

I knew about his chattiness, but hadn't recognized it as a symptom. Thinking back, my father's first meeting with my mother-in-law, Florence de Nevers, offers an example. She'd agreed to join us in an airport restaurant in San Francisco one rainy Sunday morning—we lived in Salt Lake by then. My parents and I were about to go our separate ways after visiting Kristine. My mother-in-law looked elegant as usual in spite of rubber boots over her pumps and a dripping umbrella as she eased into the circular booth. Many years a widow, she was proud of her engineer-sons and vain about her appearance. She had a house in San Francisco's Sunset District, a fine secretarial job, a dressmaker, a beautician, and several bridge clubs; she likely had not forgotten her younger son's wedding: the lack of champagne, the missing parents of the bride.

My mother, who loved everyone except Ronald Reagan—"That mutt!"— was pleased to see her and showed her the latest pictures of their mutual grandchildren. We made small talk. My father didn't miss a thing. If this woman was going to be the grand lady, he would play the fool. He answered her polite questions by talking about our town and his no-longer-working life as if it were rural Arkansas, as if we were Okies. And he praised her son, my husband, making him sound like an Einstein. "Ain't never been such a guy," he said. She seemed relieved when our departures were called.

I hadn't liked my father's hick-from-the-sticks talk. Here was one more embarrassing scene. I headed for my flight, relieved to get away.

ꝫ

After several weeks, the hospital received a long letter from my father's previous psychiatrist, Dr. Ian A. Shaw—a letter they failed to save. Dr. Shaw had treated him in the 1950s, starting with two hospitalizations at Pinel in Seattle in late 1953 and January 1954, and follow-up consultations. Dr. Shaw apparently claimed that this illness went back farther than 1953, and that the patient might have suffered from extremely bizarre delusions and hallucinations for a long time but was able to function, perhaps with medication. I only know of alcohol, his favorite tonic. My father told the doctors at Steilacoom that Dr. Shaw talked to him about something that happened when he was two years old. That puzzled him, and he said, "How could I possibly know anything about my life at that age."

But my mother had reported to the hospital's social worker that when my father was born his mother had called him "Little Mary" because she had two sons and had wanted a girl.

☙

One of the doctors wrote of my father: "he is somewhat preoccupied with religion and sexual matters too in a weird way, talking about the church and the 'little cross down here' upon which he points to his genitals."

Though it's not comfortable to contemplate my father's sexual pre-occupations, I should look at the loaded words he used to describe himself to the doctors at the hospital: "pervert," "heretic," "obsessed with religion," "voices from heaven." I don't know what sexual mores he absorbed from his Norwegian Lutheran upbringing but it could have caused him to judge his natural urges as wrong or bad. These feelings could have been amplified by a later psychosis or by an epileptic disorder. He never went to church, though the rest of us did, and it never seemed to bother him. As children we prayed for him and worried about whether he would go to heaven with us, but we didn't think of him as a heretic and hadn't judged him badly for his choice. By the time of his death, each of us had withdrawn from any church, but we never considered ourselves as heretics. Could our smug acceptance as children that ours was the only true church have made him feel like an outcast all those years? I wish the doctors at Western State had explored his religious obsession more thoroughly and written about it in their reports.

A social history taken at Steilacoom quotes Mother as saying she was "relieved to have her husband in the hospital because he had attempted suicide." She said he was definitely an introvert, that he showed a calm exterior but was suppressing emotion. He'd become "overly sensitive to criticism," and he questioned the sincerity of others. She said this suspicion of people was a recent behavior, but didn't elaborate. Had she forgotten his jealousy? Had she forgotten how he so often felt he was being followed on the drive to New York?

☙

My sister Kristine was eleven when my father became sick and she entered the precarious years of puberty as he settled deeper and deeper into his chair in the corner, into his own world. She felt insecure and was ashamed of his appearance and angry at his behavior. She couldn't wait to leave home.

One day—this would have been in about 1959—he came home and told Mother that someone downtown asked him if he planned to attend the Father-Daughter dinner being given by Kristine's high school sorority. He'd said he didn't know anything about it. Kristine had thrown away the invitation.

Mother reacted with fury as she backed Kristine into a corner: "You little shit...How could you do this to your father? Who are you to deprive him of taking his daughter to a party, who are you to decide that he won't go? How could you..."

Mother had covered for her husband's emotional insecurities for many years. This fierce reaction was totally out of character. During the war she'd maintained a climate of normalcy when he stopped talking for weeks on end, surrounding the dinner table with chatter that seemed two-sided. He'd quietly picked at his dinner or read his paper. When he became ill, she shielded him from embarrassment or disgrace—she didn't even tell her good friend Fran O'Connor where Kearny had gone when he stayed at Pinel in Seattle. Kristine and Kathy knew to say "I don't know" when asked where their father was.

When she'd come home from visiting with him in Seattle, Mother talked about the drive and the beautiful things she'd seen along the way as if she'd just returned from a pleasant trip to Frederick & Nelson department store. Did she think she was teaching her daughters to accept everything as normal?

Kristine learned the unspoken lesson: *Don't expect Daddy to be part of the family. Don't tread on his illness.*

❦

Before his hospitalization in 1962, my father drank a lot. Alcohol did ease his anxiety and may have calmed or overpowered the voices. It didn't help him sleep or soothe the pain in his legs. According to Mother his drinking had become a problem "in the last two or three years."

Young people of my father's generation had been resourceful in finding John Barleycorn, fire water, booze, hooch, whatever one likes to call strong drink, in spite of Washington's dry law of 1916 and the Volstead Act, which put the lid on alcohol sales nationally in 1919. They found out where the bootleggers operated, they made bathtub gin, and my father brewed beer from time to time. Repeal in 1933 just made access to alcohol easier.

During the Depression and the war drinking was a sport in our family. When someone dropped in, a drink promptly appeared. The print shop gave fifths of White Horse Scotch to its best customers each Christmas—I gift-wrapped many of them. Even as a fairly young child I knew some people drank a lot, and that some drinkers might be a problem: too loud, too sick, too belligerent. I always knew which of our family friends had just fallen "off the wagon," and who had been banished to Shick's, a rehabilitation hospital for alcoholics in Seattle, to dry out—again.

In our family's lean years in the late fifties and early sixties, when Mother served, again, creamed chipped beef on toast, when shoes for growing feet had to wait, when Mother parceled out partial payments to creditors, there was, somehow, still money to buy the daily fifth of bourbon.

☙

On my brief visit home that winter, I'd seen my father's painful back problem but shrugged off his mental state. I'd admired Kathy's kind concern for Daddy as she tried to fill the emotional void in the house while Mother worked. Beyond a clean oven, I hadn't contributed much to the household, and had been reluctant to look too closely at the man I thought of simply as "poor sick Daddy."

Kristine completed her sophomore year with seven months in a cold-water walk-up near Stanford's campus in Tours, France. When she arrived at the SeaTac airport that July, Mother told her they would make a stop on the way home "to pick up Daddy."

Kris said, "Where is he?"

"Western State Hospital," Mother said.

"My God, what's he doing in the looney-bin?"

My reaction would not have been as brutally honest as Kristine's.

☙

London had its Bedlam, New York had Bellevue, and we had Steilacoom! The school joke in western Washington: "You keep acting like that and it's Steilacoom for you." Early mental hospitals had names like The State Lunatic Asylum, and one of those, the ruins of Danvers, is still thought to be haunted by the witches of early Salem. We called them insane asylums,

and the word asylum held none of its possible caring, protective conno-
tations. We didn't want to believe that our father belonged in such a place.

As it turned out, after eight weeks, the hospital psychiatrists didn't
think so either. My father had not changed much during his time in the
hospital, they noted, and he was extremely homesick. The doctors thought
the benefit of a longer stay there was "somewhat dubious since he has been
psychotic off and on for at least ten years and his prognosis must be very
guarded."

He'd earned the diagnosis: "Schizophrenic reaction, paranoid type."
They gave him ten days of medications: an anti-psychotic drug related to
thorazine and an antihistamine for sleeping, but nothing for his hyper-
tension, and allowed him to go home on July 28, 1962.

How would he cope with his voices, his visions?

☙

Mother and the girls helped Daddy into the car with his suitcase and a box
of small things he'd made in the craft room. They stopped at a restaurant
for dinner. Kristine recalls that he kept talking to the waitress: "He was
bizarrely friendly." Apparently he tried to seem normal by talking to the
woman who simply wanted to take his order,

"Look at these wonderful gals," he said. "Have you ever seen such
ladies? Kristy, here, is just home from a great school. That's Stanford. The
Farm. And Buster, she's Kathy, she's my best pal. She writes the nicest
letter, she sends the prettiest pictures. She sends the peppiest news. Very
droll. And Pete..." He laughed at himself and seemed ready to go on and on,
embarrassing Kristine and Kathy, who wondered whether the hospital stay
had helped him. They drove home in silence.

My father had spent two months of confused helplessness locked up
in "Steilacoom." That place at the edge of Puget Sound, in a landscape with
the expansive elegance of a college campus, represented the only post-high
school institution he got to "attend."

☙

Could it have been lead poisoning (no, I haven't forgotten) that caused my
father's illness? He had worked with lead all the time, operating old-
fashioned equipment—the Linotype, the Ludlow—that maintained heated
reservoirs of molten lead. Often the pot was uncovered as a new ingot of
metal, called a pig, was added to it. Were lead vapors polluting the air?

Health experts try to determine what levels of lead would be harmful if found in a person's blood or tissues. Would tests have shown my father's blood contained too much lead? Symptoms of lead exposure in adults include high blood pressure which he had by the age of fifty, but so did my mother and so did I, digestive problems (I don't know), nerve disorders (his sciatica was caused by a slipped disk), cataracts (I don't think so), memory and concentration problems (does this include depression, which was a lifelong challenge for him?), muscle and joint pain (we all have some), and damage to sperm-producing organs in men (he fathered children into his forties). The list of symptoms does not include psychosis.

Sound technical reasons exist for doubting that my father suffered lead poisoning. Type metal is still made according to Gutenberg's recipe, an alloy of lead, tin, and antimony. The tin is added for hardness and to lower the melting point, the antimony to reduce shrinkage on cooling. Lead vapor would be a problem if the metal were heated to its boiling point, which is 621 degrees Fahrenheit. However, casting temperatures and remelting points in my father's machines ranged from 270 to 340 degrees Fahrenheit, a level far below the boiling point. Relieved, I can rule out lead exposure.

❦

Mother never told me everything she knew. I gave her many chances in the years before she died. I probed her memory for stories about the past, but she often changed the subject. She would tell me about the latest class she was taking at the community college (she loved history classes), or where she'd gone the day before: for example, an outing with a senior group ending at "Pet-a-llama" in Petaluma. She never mentioned seizures.

It was Mother's youngest sister, Barbara, who "spilled the beans." She claimed that Shakespeare was an epileptic, in part because he created several characters with "the falling sickness." Then she said, "You do know that your father was epileptic, don't you?" My first reaction: obviously she didn't know what she was talking about.

Then I recalled the tunnel of shimmering green water. I heard again Fran's terrifying shout that stopped me on planks in a shallow stream. Seven years my senior, Barbara might have been with us on that long-ago camping trip. Did she witness other seizure episodes? I began to listen to my brilliant aunt. A Shakespearean scholar and Emeritus Professor of English, she called often from her home in Edmonton, always eager to lay on me her current enthusiasm, discovery, or opinion. After Mother died in

1993, Barbara brought up epilepsy. She said Uncle Alec told her that on a fishing trip, he saw my father fall over a log, land face down, and then thrash and foam at the mouth. She didn't say when this happened. My father wasn't a fisherman, but Alec was, and many of our camping trips to a river or a beach would have been, for him, a fishing trip. She also said that my father engaged in long silences in their first married years, and, Barbara asserted, that was typical of an epileptic, to be silent for days on end. She said my mother would ask him, "What did I do wrong?" He wouldn't answer.

I trust many of Barbara's recollections. Newly orphaned at fourteen, she lived with us and shared my bedroom during the first year of the war, a time when my father talked little.

Barbara's research focused on the Elizabethan and Renaissance understanding of epilepsy, which included beliefs now discredited, such as the existence of an epileptic personality. Most current authorities on epilepsy no longer consider it a disease, but rather a complex of symptoms: fainting, fits, seizures, convulsions. Only recurrence of symptoms allows a diagnosis of epilepsy.

To soften her assertions, Barbara said my father was in good company, listing writers she admired, Dickens, Dostoyevsky, and Flaubert, as his brothers in epilepsy. Other famous epileptics include Alexander the Great, Caesar (Shakespeare knew this), and perhaps, Vincent van Gogh.

༚

Epilepsy is the oldest known disease of the brain, with a pedigree of four thousand years. Since antiquity, writers have claimed an association between epilepsy and mental illness. In *The Psychoses of Epilepsy*, Michael R. Trimble states that in some patients, diminished seizure frequency is followed by the onset of acute psychosis. Could this be the case with my father? The interval between his last seizure and the recognized emergence of his psychosis may have been shorter than that reported in the medical literature. However, Dr. Shaw thought that his psychotic illness started earlier than 1953.

My father told the doctors that as a young man he'd had seizures. Perhaps he'd had psychotic experiences as part of the aura or warning signal that comes at the beginning of a seizure. The seizures apparently started soon after the death of his brother Perry. He claimed that the attacks went away "ten or twenty years" before 1962. We've assumed that his psychotic episodes began with his "nervous breakdown" in 1953, which may not be true.

Kathy witnessed an incident that puts the lie on his claim of quiescence. She was ten in 1959. She and my parents were clearing out brush in the vacant lot behind our neighbor's fence, the site of our World War II victory garden, and had built a bonfire. My father fell, with a heat stroke or a seizure. There was a to-do, she recalled, and she realized later that he had probably had a seizure.

We all were puzzled and embarrassed by my father's illness; we didn't understand his behavior. I tried to ignore his altered persona. Mother totally rejected the hospital's diagnosis of schizophrenia. Where Aunt Barbara wrote with brutal honesty about her life, my mother dissembled; she always put the best face on our lives. Was she ashamed? Was she trying to protect my father's reputation, to preserve our love and respect for him? Was she in denial? I'm no better. When I heard that my father's autopsy showed old lesions in his brain, probable signs of earlier strokes, I grasped onto those unnoticed strokes to account for the change in his mental state. Wasn't it better to believe that my father suffered strokes that changed his personality, wasn't that better than having to admit he was crazy?

In spite of Mother's careful hoarding of important papers, we don't have a copy of that coroner's report. A few years ago I tried to talk to Dr. Pollock about the autopsy he performed on my father's body, to ask about the lesions he had noted. He seemed cheerful as before but his memories were vague. He didn't remember the autopsy, could say nothing about it, and instead tried at length to persuade me of the healing power of Jesus.

༄

Aunt Barbara diagnosed my father as having Temporal Lobe Epilepsy (TLE), and referred me to the 1993 study by journalist Eve LaPlante, titled *Seized*. LaPlante focused on TLE as a medical, historical and artistic phenomenon and asserted that TLE often gets misdiagnosed as schizophrenia or mood disorder.

A person afflicted with this particular syndrome of TLE, LaPlante explained, has few actual seizures, but does experience altered feelings or emotions, such as hyperreligiosity, reduced sexuality, increased aggression, stickiness—a tendency to maintain conversations longer than others might want—and hypergraphia, which is a compulsion to write or draw, hence the tie to artists and writers.[12] Other researchers note that mutism and fainting are part of TLE.

Let me count the ways my father's behavior would conform with this diagnosis. He fainted several times before going to the state hospital. I recalled being surprised by the oddly religious tone of thoughts he described to the doctors there, because he had not seemed to take religion seriously earlier in life. He told the doctors he had been impotent for six years, which Mother confirmed. All of the therapists mention that my father would talk on and on, and my sisters and I remember his tendency to engage even strangers in long, fawning conversations that were uncharacteristic and embarrassing, bizarre for an introvert. Except for the lack of compulsive writing it all seems to fit.

ã

My sisters and I worry ...Will we see tendencies of something from our "sick" father in ourselves? Some people describe the aura preceding an epileptic episode as *déjà vu*. Kristine occasionally has unusually strong feelings of *déjà vu*, but has never had a seizure. I wonder if my father had such feelings. In recent years I have experienced the aura of an ocular migraine several times, an interesting and terrifying distraction.

So now, in addition to musings about lead poisoning, I have to consider whether my father had a damaged temporal lobe. Does it make any difference to me that he might have had seizures that merely looked like epilepsy?

I'm already pulling back from reality, adopting my mother's proclivity for revising facts. Does it matter to me that my father had epilepsy? Do I prefer to think that he wasn't crazy, just damaged? In the end it doesn't matter. What remains true is that I couldn't see him. I looked away.

Epilepsy in no way defined his life. I don't believe it ever affected his ability to do his job, or to get a driver's license, or to work with mechanical equipment. I wonder whether admitting to seizures kept him out of the army during World War II—his brother Jack served, as did almost all of his brothers-in-law. I don't believe his good friends or family considered him impaired in any way before his "nervous breakdown." What I do think is that the potential for having a seizure must have terrified him.

---

[12] Geschwind Syndrome of TLE, described by Norman Geschwind, Harvard neurologist.

Though I never got to confirm any of this with my mother, I am trying to establish the facts. For too long I've accepted our family stories. I've believed them, "lock, stock and barrel," as Mother would say. I've presented her version of our family's saga as truth.

There are things I couldn't say in Mother's hearing:

My father spent time in an insane asylum.

My father had epileptic seizures. And,

My father was an alcoholic.

These statements don't alter my concern for my father, nor my wish to understand him, nor my determination to accept him as he was, and honor him.

Three Men Grilled Over Rash Of Incendiary Fires

Three men arrested in connection with a rash of incendiary fires in Aberdeen and Hoquiam early Thursday morning are being questioned by Aberdeen police and state fire marshals.

The men were arrested while Aberdeen firemen saved two downtown business buildings and rescued five persons trapped in the Pinckney apartments by one of the fires.

Questioning the men are Police Chief A. M. Gallagher, Captain John B. Gillespie, Deputy State Fire Marshals Walter Ryckman and Bruce Igou, Charles E. Landis of the National Board of Fire Underwriters, and Prosecutor James Solan.

Two of the men were released on their personal recognizance by Prosecutor Solan.

The third man, however, a 23-year-old Seattleite, was grilled until almost midnight Thursday. He claimed a lapse of memory concerning places in which he had been seen and at which fires had occurred.

The fires first came to light through a police call received at 40 minutes past 2 o'clock Thursday morning.

The call came from the apartments above the Owl pharmacy. Police were informed that a tenant in the building was holding two prowlers at bay with a butcher knife.

A minute later a fire at the apartments was reported.

When Officers Pete Popovac and Jim Foley arrived at the scene, the two prowlers were running down the stairs, with the tenant, Frank Sheele after them—brandishing his butcher knife and ordering them to stop.

Foley fired a couple of shots into the air.

The prowlers stopped.

They were taken to the police station and booked on disorderly persons charges.

Meanwhile the fire department was busy quelling the flames in the Owl apartments. The fire had been started in a second floor storeroom, and had consumed its way into two apartments.

When Foley and Popovac had completed booking the two prowlers, they left the police station by the alley entrance. On reaching H street, Foley spied a man hiding behind a truck parked near the Weatherwax apartments.

When the police car came alongside the truck, the man in hiding took off and rounded the corner and sped north along H street.

As Foley fired two shots, the man turned into the alley. There he was found hiding behind a car.

He, too, was booked as a disorderly person in connection with the fires. He makes his home in Seattle.

He is also believed to have been the third person first reported with the two prowlers caught at the Owl apartments.

The fire in the Pinckney building was reported at 3 o'clock.

This fire, too, was started in a store room at the head of the stairs. The store room was badly gutted. The flames also ate their way into a store room of the Quick Print company and into its offices, where considerable smoke and water damage was reported.

It was at the Pinckney fire where four firemen and Assistant Chief Harold Thornton rescued the five persons.

With the two fires coming upon the heels of each other, it left only four firemen to each blaze before relief arrived from a general alarm call.

Fire Chief Royce Waldrep praised the work of the eight firemen and the assistant chief, describing it as far beyond the call of duty.

One of the three men arrested is being questioned about the other fires.

One was in a rest room at the Aberdeen Eagles hall, and the other in a rest room at Gambours cafe in Hoquiam.

A fifth fire in the two communities failed to materialize.

Shortly after 8 o'clock in the morning, Barnhardt's bakery called police to report an attempt had been made to set a garage on fire at the rear of the bakery, just a half a block away from the Pinckney building.

A box of burning paper had been placed against the wall of the garage. However, the paper burned out without setting the garage on fire.

RUMMAGE SALE

The Ocosta Grange Home Economics club is holding a rummage sale this Saturday in the Community Thrift Shop annex at Wishkah and F streets, in Aberdeen, and a benefit dance tonight in the Grange hall at Bay City.

TIDEWATER BILGE

The way things are going, JIM SOLAN needs another deputy. Attention REUBEN SANDSTROM—Did you know that shovel full of asphalt landed on the east side of Myrtle street?, SPIKE HARKONEN is pretty particular about what goes on the alleys in South Aberdeen. Herr HANS SCHMIDT is going ahead full blast with his literary efforts. BILL BLUM is taking a postman's holiday. CAROLE COLLIS don't need no bear trap—Black Magic's better.

Article from Grays Harbor Post *of March 28, 1959*

The Printer's Devil

Benjamin Franklin somewhere...wrote...that hanging around a print shop was not too far from attending some fancy institution of learning, like, say, Harvard.

—Kearny Clark, 1961

Pat O'Connor may have seemed an unlikely hero, but he earned the title. Standing tall at 5'8", he lacked his father's rugged good looks, but he did inherit the old man's charm and his weakness for booze. Even at sixty, with his smooth skin and a crewcut, in spite of a few extra pounds, he projected a youthful and carefree demeanor. As a girl I would have described him as silly, abashed, endearing; later as overly affectionate—any woman who'd sat next to him in a restaurant booth knew what I meant—a flatterer, a clever card dealer, undependable in his drinking years, but always, a committed friend to the Clarks.

His parents, Fran and Bill O'Connor, had known mine since their high school years, both as neighbors and friends, so he and I had to get along. We tagged along on picnics and camping trips, birthdays and holiday parties. We grew up together, but reacted differently to things. A class ahead of me in school, he liked to joke and tease. Raised to be prim and proper, I lacked a sense of humor. He didn't much like school, I always had my hand raised with the answer. He was thrown out of St. Mary's for chewing gum, while I flew blithely through all eight grades with the nuns on a carpet of "A"s. I went off to college and never lived in Aberdeen again. He spent most of his life on Grays Harbor. Only in recent years have I realized how much we had in common. We honored the past, we hoarded family memories, and we shared a fondness for my printer father. We both felt nostalgia for the old hot metal print shop.

My junior year in high school, I invited Pat to be my escort for a girl's-choice dance sponsored by my high school sorority. He seemed to me a safe choice since neither of us went out much and obviously we were just friends. Lest I'd forgotten, this dance date is one of the many events in my young life documented in the *Post's* society notes. For the United States, the *New York Times* has always been understood to be a newspaper of record; for my family, the *Grays Harbor Post* was suitably authoritative enough to be our newspaper of record.

Pat O'Connor may not have been a great student, but he learned quickly. He enjoyed recounting how he got his first job. In the new Effective Living Course in high school, its title much ridiculed by our parents, he chuckled, the teacher sent the students out to interview a business man. Pat went down to Quick Print to interview the business man he knew best, my father. He asked him to talk about the printing business and "Kearny handed me a broom!" Pat earned seventy-five cents an hour for sweeping out at the end of the day, and he paid attention. By his senior year he left school an hour early every day to work at the shop. Like my father, or perhaps learning from him, Pat could tinker with machines and keep them working. He soon became a pressman and poured the hot lead for the stereotype machine, a typical duty for a printer's devil. One year his cousin Bunny got a job selling ads for the paper. Pat said, "Kearny was great, he would give anybody a job." As I well knew.

Pat worked at the shop most of its final fifteen years. Toward the end, when my father struggled, Pat took up the slack. After the second fire, he helped move the business, then bought it. Unbeknownst to me, he held onto my father's printing lessons until that book signing in 1995, which gave him top billing on my list of heroes.

༃

When was that second fire? It had to have been after I left home. Kristine's memories of the shop straddle the transition to the new location. She did some proofreading in the old shop: "up those steep stairs, stinking of a combination of tobacco smoke, ink and grease." Sometime before she went off to college in the fall of 1960, she also did some work in the new building. "There was something pathetic about having to move into a church," she said. Pat and my father put the paper's last issue on the press at the new location in January, 1961.

The microfilm record must save the day. Again lighting it up and threading in the skimpy roll of the last year of the *Post*, I scanned quickly, and almost missed the account of a fire in the issue dated March 28, 1959. The front-page story: "Three Men Grilled over Rash of Incendiary Fires" didn't look very interesting until I noted that the shop, *our shop*, fell victim to one of them. In the early hours of March 26, the Aberdeen Fire Department responded to a call from the Owl Pharmacy downtown. At 3 am, someone reported a second fire, this time in the Pinkney Building, where the shop rented space above the plumbing business. The fire started in a storeroom at the head of the stairs, a stairway never locked because it gave access to a narrow hallway of apartments. The storeroom blazed fiercely. The story continued: "The fire then ate into the stockroom of Quick Print Co.," causing much smoke and water damage. My old fortress of paper, violated, again.

Drama unfolded that night. According to the account, the Fire Department "rescued 5 persons from the Pinkney Apartments," whose exit was blocked by fire. I imagine scared people in their nightshirts, one after another, clambering out onto the tall ladders, escorted to safety in the middle of G Street. Three smaller fires that night keep the firemen busy. Only after reading this story did I noticed that this issue of the *Post* consisted of only four pages. My father could ill afford to miss a deadline; the issue contained some news and the legal notices which by law and contract had to be published in a timely manner, and little else.

The fire left behind a dismal scene. Pat said he and Kearny talked about conditions in the shop being so bad that, if they wanted the business to survive and continue for some years, they should move out of the ageing second story space. In order to buy new type and two used presses, my father mortgaged the house we had owned free and clear for twenty-six years. In hindsight, cancelling the paper then and downsizing the printing business might have been a better idea, but that was a decision my sick father was unable to make.

☙

The move out of the Pinkney building presented challenges. Pat found the only crane in town and hired it to hoist the heavy equipment out the double doors above the alley. A used press just large enough to print the paper came to the new location from the *Longview Daily News*. But my father wouldn't give up the huge Babcock flatbed press he and his brother had bought just before Jack went off to war. He patiently took the cumbersome machine apart, rupturing several of his spinal disks in the process, and they lowered it in pieces in order to cart them to the new building.

"Your dad was in love with the big press," Pat said. My father never got to reassemble it in the crowded space of the former chapel. Later, when he owned the business, Pat called Western Steel to haul the carcass away as scrap.

Recently I asked Pat if he minded going back over all these memories. "It's OK, honey," he said. "I been dreaming about it all. Around election time you would feel a strain, maybe not conscious, but it was always there. The dream, it's always the same. It's the day before the election, and we hadn't printed the ballots yet...You didn't get drunk or anything. But it was a strain."

꠲

In truth, nothing could have saved the *Grays Harbor Post*. The move to a new location only delayed the decision. Lacking timely advertisements and an editorial presence, the paper lost its readership. The era of the traditional weekly paper had run its course.

One terrible day just after New Year's in 1961, my father sat down at his typewriter to write to his readers for the first time in seven-and-a-half years. He would have to confess to failure.

To reconstruct this painful episode, I scrounged in Mother's cardboard expanding file again, looking for financial records, any kind of evidence to help understand the why and wherefore of this decision. In among a number of colorful stock certificates from long-defunct, pre-World War II oil drilling and mining companies and more recent health insurance records, I *found* something overlooked: a neatly bound report from the family's accountant and two years' income tax statements for the years in question. The home and business were one entity.

Not surprisingly the financial report showed that the printing business eked out income barely above poverty level for a family of four—there were still two daughters at home. During these years Mother took in boarders, including two unladylike women who got on my father's nerves. Mother's salary for her work in Dr. Bryant's office apparently appeared elsewhere. The *Post* contributed almost nothing to the shop's bottom line but required staff to put it out.

Still in constant pain from the injury incurred in the move and in spite of voices that may have roiled in his head, my father pounded out a notice to appear in a black-bordered box at top center of page one of the January 21, 1961 issue of the *Post*:

Notice

Any time a business can survive under one continuing management for a period of 57 years, it can only do so as a result of many strong associations of friendship and loyalty.

As such is certainly true in our case, you may well appreciate the distaste and utter repugnance we here of the Grays Harbor Post feel as we submit this announcement of the End of The Grays Harbor Post, the last publication set for January 28th [1961].

A heartbreaking story. I wonder whether *he* kept a dry eye as he tried to comfort his readers: "There is no need to shed tears for a vanished institution..." and promised to preserve the *Post*'s morgue as a valuable historical reference. He knew that morgue would be cared for. The fifty-seven volumes of news and features are still accessible, in large part because the newspaper's glossy book stock holds up and displays photographs well. The full collection is maintained by the Aberdeen Timberland Library, on microfilm by the state of Washington, and in both forms in my guestroom closet.

A week later, for the last issue he wrote a full-length editorial that began:

God knows...
That when you attempt to take a modest and honorable approach to signing off a weekly newspaper after 57 years of effort, more or less, on the face of it there really isn't much to say.

He mentioned Benjamin Franklin's assertion that "hanging around a print shop was not too far from attending some fancy institution of learning, like, say, Harvard.... We don't lay a lot of claims to any education, but hanging around our shop hasn't left too much to be desired...." He claimed to have learned a lot from back-shop philosophers who also turned out "remarkably fine printing." He ruminated about the talents of the previous editors, his father and brother, who would disapprove of his decision to quit publication, and of the columnists. He concluded by talking about his failures as a businessman and editor:

We are not much of a hand at needling anybody. In fact we like to leave that to the other guy. But 57 years in this business does give us the right to hand down to our kids one little thought which we'll express right here. Sometimes we run into folks who think everybody else needs their clock cleaned, but it's usually their ever-loving customers who eventually do the clock-cleaning where it was needed ever so badly in the first place. That being so, this outfit signs off with no regrets whatsoever. In that well known and time-hallowed tradition: Ain't it just too bad?

The last editorial is disappointing because it was rambling and disorganized, though not unexpectedly so. I don't understand what he wanted to tell us kids in the last paragraph. But I recognize the last line, the title of a 1935 Gene Gifford song often recorded by Glen Gray. I can see my father hunker down in his chair in the corner, a tumbler of golden liquid and ice cubes in hand, playing the record over and over and over on the old turntable. Tomorrow he must write his swan song. His days as a publisher, over. Too bad, too bad. And soon, too soon, he will have to give up the printing business. He has let his father down. *Ain't it just too bad?*

☙

My father retired after thirty years at age fifty-three with a small annuity from the Printer's Union, but he knew he would miss the smell of ink and the soothing sounds of a printing press, so he offered to help out at his old shop. Pat tried to keep the printing business going, and recalled, "We had an under-the-table-deal that Kearny would come in and do Linotype work for me." Pat couldn't always count on his former boss to show up, Kearny was unpredictable. "One day," after a week or two of working for him, Pat said, "Kearny went over to the *Aberdeen World* newspaper print shop and turned in his time." He must have been confused. He couldn't keep track of who he worked for, or of what the under-the-table-deal meant. Here was further evidence of my father's mental state. This episode got Pat in trouble with the union and he could no longer let Kearny work. After hiring as printer the teacher who had taught him printing at the high school, Pat learned to run the Linotype. Things came to a standstill, he recalled, while he sat at "that damn machine" setting the *Ocean Breeze* or type for ballots and other jobs.

Pat's friend and nearby business man, Don Spoon, came over one day and said to him, "You know what you've been doing all these years, Pat. You're burned out trying to keep Kearny alive."

The transition to some kind of voting machine also cut into his business, Pat recalled. "Paper ballots were better. They were honest. The people [working the polls] were so conscientious, so it was the most honest system. Now nobody knows everybody."

He kept the print shop going on his own for about six years. As more mills shut down, only "piddling jobs" came in his door, letterhead, accounts payable stuff, menus, jobs not worth much. He finally sold the big press to Hoquiam's *Washingtonian* newspaper and the rest of the equipment to our by-then-divorced uncle Alec Dunsire, who, in 1959, left our troubled shop and set up one of his own.

Pat said, "I always thought if I had any artistic talent I should get into offset printing. Ours was all mechanical. The offset folks were cutting [our prices] in half. We were between a rock and a hard place. Offset wasn't that good then and it was expensive to convert. We always did quality printing, wouldn't compromise. They could take our stuff and copy it...It was the end of an era, that's what it amounted to."

℮

Pat may have carried a torch for me all these years. He always found out when I was coming to visit Aberdeen or the beach. In the 1990s he came to the cocktail party at a reunion of my class, just to see me. A pleasing and flattering experience. A faithful friend who still felt the bond between our families, as did I.

One summer visit to the old town, friend Sharyn and I picked him up to go to lunch in Tokeland. He chatted cheerily in spite of the usual grey Harbor weather, the noticeable moisture in the air. Though he seemed not to have a care in the world, Pat claimed he found cities stressful. He was living in a motel unit in Westport, a beachy village on the coast west of Aberdeen, where he kept the grounds, the lawn, and the flowers for the owner. The quiet life suited him. He recalled my family in the old days. "The saddest thing is when Jack died. He and Kearny were perfect partners.

Kearny was happy to be in the back shop, Jack was happy to be the bullshitter. Things could have been different if..."

I heard in Pat's voice the familiar family narrative. As one of our family's oldest, and oldest surviving, friends, one who stayed in town in the years after I left home, he knew what he was talking about. His loyalty to my father, to my family, touched me.

"That's what's wrong with all these wars, they take the good guys."

The weathered New-England-severe shingled building of the hundred-year-old Tokeland Hotel stood on what's left of the sandy point at the north shore of Willapa Harbor. We welcomed the warmth of the homey dining room, the view of mossy grass, a few brave petunias in sandy flowerbeds.

Over lunch, as we talked about my father, the print shop, and Pat's life, I watched a steady downpour bounce off the roof of a small gazebo. Because I'd lived in Utah's desert for many years, I mentioned that I enjoyed a good rain. "It's just a mist," he said.

His conversation moved back to the shop. "The pressmen always joked that Kearny was going to start a fire," he said. "The sink was behind the big press, and it always had a leaky faucet; Kearny would go back to shut it off or try to fix it, and in passing, pop his pipe out in the ashcan. All it would take is a few hot coals...." The first fire did start in that corner, ignited spontaneously in a pile of inky cleaning rags, according to the investigators.

It felt right to be with Pat on a beach day, to hear his stories. He had a remarkable memory for names and details. When he tilted his head and gave that self-conscious smile, I saw again the grinning boy fidgeting in frames of Uncle Jack's home movies, eager to get away from the center of attention all those years ago. He put his arm around me as we walked back to the car with the mist in our faces, tasting the sea.

Kearny Clark's faithful Corona portable

✐ Last Hurrah

Your old man's about washed up!
—Kearny Clark, 1965

I spoke too soon in declaring that my father exhibited no signs of hypergraphia or compulsive writing. After a spring's random attic cleaning, I found another box of old Christmas cards and letters, untidy, unlabeled, dusty. Lo and behold, among them were some letters written to me by my father in his last years. Several reminded me of an almost-forgotten visit with my family and with him.

My parents and Kathy came to visit us in Salt Lake City, where we settled after living briefly near Los Angeles. Mother's sister Peggy proudly drove the four of them across the rivers and mountains of Oregon and the plain of Idaho in her yellow Fury hardtop, an excess of 1960s fins and chrome. By that July of 1965 we had been in our house only nine months and were in the midst of several do-it-yourself projects at once: renovating the basement, cleaning out the small side-yard, and building a fence to give it privacy. Recent arrivals in Utah, we decided to take my family to the desert, not realizing it would make a better spring or fall outing.

❦

We camped in the bottom loop of Devil's Garden, the Arches National Park campground, a fairyland of red sandstone fins that I've since come to love. But that summer day, as newcomers to the desert, we saw only barren sand, a juniper or two, and little else where we'd camped next to tall hunks of raw rock. We straggled back into our campsite under a clear blue sky and a hot sun and found little shelter. Our visitors from the Pacific Northwest were used to a landscape carpeted in moss, evergreens dripping from a recent rain, cool moist air from the sea. They were miserable. We'd cut short our hike when my father, not used to walking on uneven ground over rocky trails and along natural washes, twisted his ankle. We huddled in a pool of shade wishing it *were* a pool and decided to leave first thing next day. The only comfort came after a beautiful sunset. When the evening turned chilly, Mother built a small fire, and my father stretched out on the sandy slope beside it with a beer. We set out our sleeping bags and he admired the night sky. Just as it had been in my childhood summers when he took us camping every weekend, the night sky would be our canopy, and here, it was gorgeous.

I heard him say, "Gosh, the stars. I haven't seen this many since El Paso.... I still remember the bedbugs in that hole...." Stars punctured the dark dome above us all the way down to the horizon. I recalled nights outdoors growing up. We kids liked to camp out on the lawn after a rare dry, sunny summer day as the sky shaded into midnight blue from east to west. I had seen a faint Milky Way only once.

That night in Arches, the Milky Way wasn't just a wispy cloud, it ran in two amazingly bright streaks north to south directly overhead. I could almost feel us spinning out into space at the edge of the galaxy.

My father came to life. He repeated things I'd become accustomed to hearing: "You guys are the greatest! What a swell life you have...Your kids are real live-wires, great little hikers... That Noel is something special." As usual he put himself down, saying, "Your old man is about washed up." I thought that too, but didn't say so. His ankle probably bothered him. Sleeping on the hard ground would surely kick up the sciatica left over from his back injury, but he stayed cheerful, claiming he was, "sure glad to be here." He would never give advice, though if he thought some was called for, it came as something his father said to him, for example: "My dad used to tell us to try to do the right thing, to do the best you can."

We were strivers, Noel and I, pushing all the time to get more done in an hour, in a day. I seldom slowed down. Even in high school, I tried to do everything. If I collapsed with a cold or a blue funk and stayed home from school, Mother described me in nautical language: "Nancy has only two speeds: full speed ahead or full stop." In those first Utah years I had three children, an old house, and a high-achieving husband to keep up with. Full speed ahead, indeed.

After the abbreviated camping trip we took our guests to an outdoor performance of *Aida* with live-horse-drawn chariots, then started on projects in the side yard and the basement. Aunt Peggy and Mother helped my husband dig holes and set fence posts in concrete. My father helped him do the rough-in for a new shower stall in the basement and installed some wiring. To confound the mix, my mother-in-law and a friend of hers offered to visit while they were in town, so we would have to clean up and try to look presentable after a day of chores. We assigned sixteen-year-old Kathy to the kitchen, asking her to produce a turkey dinner with all the trimmings. My mother-in-law, who may have looked askance on my hardworking family, smiled graciously and even asked for the recipe for my father's favorite dish, scalloped corn. Mother as usual commented that "Kearny will eat any vegetable as long as it is corn."

That cool night sitting in the sand beside my exhausted father remains one of the few times in those years that I relaxed and paid attention to him. Mostly I thought of him as a doddering old man. He was actually only fifty-seven and could still wield a hammer, handle a screwdriver, and pound a mean typewriter, as it turns out.

❦

That last box from the attic contained several affectionate, relatively lucid letters from my father written about the time of his visit to Utah. These chatty letters are a pleasant surprise because we know now that he wrote no editorials after the ill-fated trip to New York. Aunt Barbara's argument that he suffered from a kind of Temporal Lobe Epilepsy had been weakened by his lack of compulsive writing. However, I now must acknowledge that in his last years, with time on his hands, daytimes in a quiet house, a supply of paper, and his faithful Corona on a typewriter table, he often rolled a sheet into the old machine and typed letters that make up in a small way for the missing editorials.

He composed at the keyboard of the old typewriter with the green ribbon using the kind of newsprint he formerly used for copy and proofs in the print shop. Unlike printed material, his typed output was uneven— letters struck by the weak fingers of the left hand were less distinct than others. Mother's letters found in this same box were handwritten until she mastered typing while working in a doctor's office and found she could bootleg time to write while the Doctor was out.

In one letter my father wrote about my February visit home over Valentine's week. I studied the date on the letter. Actually it was months later, and he had just come home from Steilacoom, but he made no mention of having been away. He thanked me "for coming up to take care of the old goat when he was non-operational." He'd had an operation; did he intend the pun? He sat down to write because he wanted to explain how my sister

Kathy, then thirteen, would be arriving by train to visit us in Los Angeles, and he was concerned that I might not know how to find her. He wrote confusing details about the schedule for the Southern Pacific's "elite train," the *Lark*, and suggested I talk to a Mr. Hanson so "there is no hitch" in meeting her. "Buster has been counting the days and minutes over this trip...." and "Buster...is one hell of a good friend of mine." Since he wasn't working, he knew he would miss her around the house: "She sure leaves a gap at home." I shrugged off the letter—just dithering Daddy—and as he predicted in the closing line, figured out how and when to meet Kathy at the main train station.

Nothing Daddy could write in that era would disabuse me of my image of him as someone beyond the pale.

For a man who stopped writing editorials in 1953, he became almost prolific. Another letter recalls our night in the desert. "How much we enjoyed our visit in Utah," he wrote. "I was really chagrined when I sprained that ankle as I know the Arches was worth every bit of the walk." He mentioned that I am lucky to be "in such a healthy, dry climate." He remembered the campsite, how we felt surrounded by ghost rocks. "What the ages have done shows up so spectacularly in that desert air...everything tends to preserve itself there, just like our forest country shows what nature can grow in the way of wood in a couple of thousand years."

Another letter again recalled his visit to Salt Lake City, mentioning, "the fun working on the grape stake fence." "Sure wish I could be helping with that basement [remodeling]—I learn so much from what Noel knows about cement, electric circuit-testing and all." He thought he would need help from my husband on the planned beach house: "If I ever get to wiring our tool shed out at the beach I'll have to ask Noel for a diagram of the hook-up."

These letters put the lie to my contention that he was a demented or out-of-it father. I can't have paid much attention to them. I wish I had taken more time to look at him when he visited here, to savor his compliments, to listen to his aches and pains, his mulling over of what life was about. I regret that all I have is the recollection of a fleeting fireside under our desert's stunning sky. I couldn't know it would be the last time we would be together, the last time to connect.

In three letters from '65 and '66 he writes cheerily about the beginning of a building project at Cohassett Beach. In spite of everything—his illness, their financial straits—my parents decided to join with Mother's sister, Peggy, and her husband, Jen, to build a house on land J.W. Clark had bought years before, land my family had paid taxes on for years. Though not as strong as when he built our garage, he was clearly delighted that he would be confronted with tasks he could do, that he had done years before: working with his hands, measuring, sawing, hammering, building forms for a foundation, helping tamp cement into them, cutting plates for the tops of the foundation, framing walls. In several letters he again mentioned that he would like to pick my husband's brain on wiring, because he had never wired a 220-volt service for heating uses.

In another letter, mentioned in my visit to Fort Worden, he relived shooting the big gun during his National Guard encampments years before. I'm glad that he felt he could boast about his guard duty while writing to his oldest grandson. He sent a medal he had earned, but I don't know whether my son kept it. The dimpled silver trophy from that service, inscribed: "1928 Efficiency Trophy won by Private Kearney [sic] Clark 248th A.D." lies tarnishing in two pieces in the archival box where I found these letters. My legacy to my children will be the welter of memories and memorabilia of my life and my father's, and his father's, wonderfully jumbled together along with similar things from my mother's family, going back to the diary of her third great grandfather. A legacy of "treasures" that four generations haven't been able to throw away.

☙

In his next, last letter, my father described the beginnings of the beach project, an attack on "Camp Swampy." Truckloads of sand had been dumped in the low places in their beach lot, in the hope that the winter rains would help settle it. They planned to start in the spring to build a small utility building and then the house. On their recent visit they found "the joint is just about flooded,...we are surrounded by a moat and even awash in spots." He and Uncle Jen dug a ditch, which "started to take the top of the lake off ..., [we] are going to dig another ditch that should just about empty a lake covering a good 150 yards square. We care not where that water goes but we'll hear about it no doubt. But it isn't our water so we'll let someone else figure it out."

The beach house project really gave him a lift, a new lease on life, Kathy remembered. He and my mother drove to the beach often to look at the property. On one of those trips they stopped in to see Kathy Hogan, whose newspaper columns my father had published in the *Grays Harbor Post* during the 1940s. They must have left young Kathy at home. He wrote, "Kathy Hogan proceeded to ply us with 100-proof bourbon and we ended up at the fancy Islander [restaurant] out at the Cove and hit it up until 12...Man, do those gals, Grandma [my mother] and Kathy, have a good time. Kathy is one of the greatest...While everybody else was contributing to the fun, for some reason the back legs of my stool gave out and did I do a backward somersault. Somebody has to be the buffoon I guess."

He didn't seem worried that I would think less of him for telling this story about himself. Relieved that the three of them hadn't been thrown out of the place, he commented, "Such grandparents! Tsk, tsk...." I marvel that they managed to take Kathy home and drive the twenty miles back to Aberdeen.

In early spring, the kit for the whole project arrived from Lindahl Cedar Homes, and they began building the two structures. When the small outbuilding was completed, my father moved in with a cot and his tools, so he'd have more time to work on the house. My mother and Aunt Peggy and Uncle Jen came on weekends. By July they had almost completed the exterior of the house and begun the framing for the bedrooms and bath. My father had started to install the electric wiring, a task he found challenging.

Busy with our own projects, we hadn't planned to visit that summer of 1966. We hadn't expected to be there to pitch in on their project. I wouldn't get to see my father puttering with his carpenter's folding tape measure, the T-square, a pencil behind his ear, a cold pipe clenched in his teeth. I wouldn't get to smell the fresh sawdust that fell below the sawhorses as he trimmed two-by-fours, the salt air, the scent of fried potatoes as one of my aunts took her turn as camp cook.

I can only imagine the pleasure he took in careful work, how pleased he was to see the house slowly grow on its footings.

I was not there the morning he woke to what must have been a crushing pain. I did not see him fall off his cot, his head strike the floor.

Not there with Kathy to call for help, or try to make him comfortable. Or to go with him in the ambulance the twenty miles to the hospital.

I wasn't there.

*Clark and Anderson marker
in Fern Hill Cemetery, Aberdeen*

Tearing Down the Chase

I know of no evidence to support the view that "public" viewing of an embalmed body is somehow "therapeutic" to the bereaved.
— Jessica Mitford, *The American Way of Death*

Scrubbed by a midnight thunderstorm, the air sparkled under blue skies that hot July day in Salt Lake City when I answered the first phone call. Kathy relayed the news of a stroke. I alerted my husband and tried to get a seat on a plane to Seattle. Because of an airline strike there were no flights. The second call caught me in the laundry room. I would be too late. Huddled on the floor, my back against the washer, feet propped on the dryer, I wept.

But just for a bit.

I had to get home to help Mother and Kathy. I had to finish the laundry, so my husband and the children could pack up and follow by car in a few days. I had to go sit at the airport in hopes of getting on a flight. I had to listen to Aunt Peggy, who met me in Seattle, go on about how it was my mother's fault, she shouldn't have left a weak, sick man alone at the beach. Peggy repeated that litany as she drove the long road to Aberdeen where I found Mother dry-eyed and impassive.

I felt for her. She may have had mixed emotions, but she would miss him. They had enjoyed working on the new house. She would not have the chance to share it with him, they would not be together to see his grandchildren grow up, and I knew that would be hard.

My feelings for my father had long been enclosed in a carefully wrapped box labeled *disdain*. There were other words graffitied on the box, as well: *scorn, rejection, disregard, embarrassment, and contempt.* Love and affection were sealed inside. I was not ready to unwrap a package held so firmly closed by pride and practicality. Now I no longer had a father. I wouldn't mourn.

☙

Daddy had loved to take the family, or anyone who would go with him, for a drive. He wore his battered felt hat, clutched a pipe in his teeth, and rested his arm on the doorframe. The window was always open, even when it rained. The pipe often burned out, and he'd one-handedly thrust it into the bag of tobacco in his pocket, then tamp the contents down with his thumb and try to relight it. On a rainy day, the Chrysler's top would be up, and as the years passed and the canvas failed, we'd feel moisture spitting in and running like tears down our faces.

~

My sisters were quiet as our brother Phil drove us down the hill in the family car. Because of the airline strike, it had taken several days to get us all to town. It felt like the first time we had come together to do anything, certainly the first time since we'd become adults. Kristine and Kathy could really be thought a "second family." Phil went away to college just after Kathy's birth and I left for college two years later, so the two girls spent most of their childhood without older siblings. Kathy had felt some confusion—once when I'd come home for summer vacation, then three-year-old Kathy told the mailman, "Oh yes, both Mammas are home."

Phil pulled the car into the mortuary's covered driveway next to a black hearse and we entered the somber, carpeted, and muffled world of the undertaker. I soon realized that this establishment aimed to do more than comfort hapless people like us, it looked after its profit margins. Had I expected them to operate like a charity? As a bereaved daughter I expected to be treated with respect.

The colorless Whiteside son, Gene Jr., greeted us. He had been a schoolmate of ours—I knew him as Buddy, an unlikely nickname for such a remote-seeming person. I don't remember who started the conversation. He took over. He knew how to talk about his business without reminding us that our father's cold body waited in the embalming room below. He seemed sure that we would want to "invest" in a beautiful service, a comfortable casket. Nothing about what the coffin was really for. Why did it need to be "comfortable?" He appealed to our pride: the selection we made would show how much we respected our father, would demonstrate to his friends what a fine man he had been; it would impress strangers.

He lead us through the rooms displaying elaborate options—enormous coffins of highly polished wood or embossed metal, with beveled corners, chrome fittings, quilted cushions of white satin—everything seemed too fancy for burying our unpretentious father who cared nothing for fancy clothes, who made fun of our clothier neighbor who had a different and appropriate outfit for each household chore. My father would chide Mother when she wanted him to get "dolled up" in a suit: "You can't make a silk purse out of a sow's ear." I began to worry about the cost of things, and asked for numbers.

The printer's union provided a burial fund, but we didn't know how big it was. Gene would probably have known, I later realized. Mother had kept up a small life insurance policy with tiny installments paid to an unctuous agent who visited almost weekly over the years. I had an inkling, later confirmed, that the family's finances were precarious. We could not choose a fancy coffin.

My brother said little. He was a Lieutenant Commander in the Navy's submarine service stationed in Hawaii and didn't want to embarrass himself in front of a schoolmate. He didn't like to have anyone think he couldn't afford the best. He cringed as I told Gene our father would have wanted to be buried in a simple pine box and asked whether there weren't a less expensive choice.

Whiteside said, "Oh, you mean the 'Welfare Coffin.'"

He didn't have one on the floor to show us. My siblings said nothing. "Do you not have one?" I asked. "Oh, yes," he said. But it would have to be brought up from the basement.

"We'll wait," I said.

Kristine and Kathy slumped into chairs in the showroom. Having left home to college and a marriage in California, Kristine didn't trust her feelings and spaced out of the whole experience. Seventeen-year-old Kathy was grieving. She had been rooming next door at the O'Connors' in Cohassett because of a summer job at the fishing dock, and it was she who found Daddy. She felt terrible that she had not gotten to him sooner.

Whiteside took us back to a poorly lit room far away from satin pillows and silk linings. The "welfare coffin" appeared plain but acceptable. After its few public moments, wasn't it going into the ground? As we concluded the paperwork, we were told that the charges included the cost of a concrete vault to house the coffin in order to prevent slumping of the grave's turf. Even the most opulent coffins incurred this addition. I had thought that filling in any collapse would have been part of what the cemetery called "Perpetual Care," a cost we also incurred.

The funeral would take place on Saturday. Some of us decided to head to the beach to look at the unfinished house. Mother asked to stop at the mortuary on the way. I stayed in the car. After quite a while, she returned, pale and quiet, carrying a package of personal effects. Mother's good friend Fran O'Connor also came out, chided us for not going in, and said, "He looks fine, like he is resting peacefully."

～

As a child growing up, I didn't consider that my father might have been born a melancholic. I made excuses for him. He was the victim of circumstances: I assumed he was unhappy because he hadn't saved his oldest brother from drowning; that he lost his identity because his mother didn't recognize him after that death; that his stomach churned because his father was too stern and demanding (I don't know what went on in that woodshed he sometimes mentioned); I thought he drank too much because his brother Jack didn't come home from the war; that he felt overwhelmed and unable to cope because he didn't like having to run the family business; that he had an inferiority complex because he had felt outclassed by two older brothers, who could do everything better and went to college and were gregarious and could easily reach out to others. I did know that he found comfort in trombone and saxophone laments and New Orleans blues. I saw him pour himself consolation from Old Grandad.

His anguish. Now over.

～

The funeral parlor provided a small chapel, a space bereft of any religious symbol or icon. The coffin stood alone, and open, in the front of the room and many friends and neighbors filled chairs behind it. We of the family sat in a sequestered space in the back, behind a filmy curtain. I'd seen a lot of funerals conducted in St. Mary's Church a few blocks away. In my "Sisters'-School" years I sang with the choir for many Requiem High Masses, as did my sisters later. There the bereaved family sat in the front pews and pall bearers brought the flower-bedecked (and closed) coffin to the front of the center aisle at the start of the mass. The plaintive Gregorian chants, the priest's droning of garbled passages from the missal, and the ritual incense swirling about the casket gave a sense of finality and dignity to the ceremony. Even from our enforced purdah we could see that this was going to be different.

My father's service felt like a meeting of the Kiwanis, or a music recital but with the surreal aura of a carnival freak show (that cadaver on the stage). There were organ renditions of "Going Home," "Joy of Man's Desire" [*sic*] and "A Mighty Fortress." We might have preferred some mumbled but comforting *Panis Angelicus* or a *Requiescat in pace*, some of the sung and spoken Latin phrases Daddy had teased us about.

As a child he attended the Norwegian Lutheran Church. He'd agreed to have his Justice-of-the-Peace marriage blessed by a priest a month into it, and didn't protest when Mother enrolled us, one by one, in the Catholic School. He sometimes joked about how he would go down to fire and brimstone when he died, and as children we prayed for his soul.

The service was officiated by Rev. Donald Miller, a minister we'd met the night before. He hadn't known my father and failed to remember the names of all his children, for which Kristine, the one he forgot, long held a grudge. My father would have been happier to have had an official from the printers' union, or his old friend, John Forbes, talk about the man I chose to remember, the man with ink-stained hands locking up a form for the big press, the printer who composed editorials at the console of the Linotype, the quiet guy who loved his work, his family, his friends.

It wasn't possible to get things right. In her dazed condition, Mother asked Forbes to write the obituary and was saddened later to notice things he left out.

Riding in the limousine to the cemetery, I had *déjà vu*, my body registering similar trips when I was the four-year-old or the six-year-old in my Sunday clothes perched on a fold-down jump seat facing veiled and somber relatives. I wondered if Mother also recalled the years when my grandparents, and one of hers, died, a time about which she said simply, "There were a lot of funerals."

Death had come to the last of my father's family—the last of J.W. Clark's sons—and I couldn't grieve. My father had lived with bereavement, with rejection, with loss, with mental illness. Now it was over for him. At least I should honor his memory and acknowledge this, I should feel, and express sorrow. But that day I chose to be efficient and rational. I clung to anger and resentment, and identified a convenient target, the undertaker.

Friends, neighbors, and Mother's sisters set out an ample funeral lunch. Other friends surrounded Mother wishing to comfort her. Finally our neighbor Dr. Pollock escorted her to a comfortable chair in the yard where he checked her blood pressure and prescribed rest and medication.

ॐ

As people began to leave, Gene Whiteside arrived with the floral displays from the chapel. I followed him back to his car in the driveway. I told him his label for the lowest-cost coffin was offensive. "We all know the mortuary isn't giving the coffin away. We aren't a charity case," I said. "What you called that coffin is unfriendly and unkind. You shame people into spending more than they can afford." As he started moving toward his car, I had more to say. "It is cruel and insensitive to force a family to have to choose something called a 'welfare' box."

I enjoyed the adrenaline rush, being assertive, articulate, angry. I didn't worry about hurting the feelings of my listener.

Gene looked surprised, as if he weren't used to having a woman, a girl, he probably thought even though we were the same age, speak so angrily to him. His job was to console, not to apologize. He tried to get away as quickly as he could. I enjoyed watching the struggle as he maneuvered his limousine backward and forward inches at a time in our crowded driveway to finally make his way up the hill.

ॐ

The outpouring of sentiment when my father died was notable. Mother saved cards, letters, and tags from floral donations, noted who brought food for the wake, and who offered memorial masses to be said in his behalf. She recorded the thoughtfulness of friends, neighbors, and family in the mortuary's remembrance book. Later she made a checkmark beside each name as she worked through the list writing thank-you notes, a task more wrenching than the funeral itself.

My father's then-psychiatrist lamented that the loss came at a time when my father "was happier and more active." His earlier psychiatrist, Dr. Shaw, had admired "Mr. Clark...his quiet dignity, courage and unfailing consideration of others even in the face of all his problems and pain." My father's one female cousin, Mildred, wrote, "We kept meaning to drive down to Aberdeen to see you." Brother-in-law Freddie said, "I'll miss Kearny more than I would most of my brothers and sisters."

ॐ

After the funeral we pitched in to work on the partly-finished beach house. My husband picked up where my father had left off and completed the wiring in several rooms. Phil's wife Ann and I stapled insulation between the studs of the outside walls. Phil completed the rough plumbing for the kitchen and bathroom, and built a long cedar trestle table. Then we went back to our lives, leaving the rest to Mother and Peggy and Jen.

My father didn't get to admire the final project. He didn't have a chance to sit by the fire in the beach house. Nor did he get to look out the south-facing windows to watch a fog bank roll over the dune and swallow up the beach willows and pines in the yard.

ॡ

Back in Utah several weeks after the funeral, I devoured Jessica Mitford's 1963 bestseller, *The American Way of Death*, and became even angrier with what Mitford described as the "macabre euphemisms" of the profiteering funeral industry. I read with horror the vivid details in her "exquisitely disgusting" description of the embalming room.[13] I had not gone to view my father's embalmed body. I'd not had to think of what gruesome hoses and tubes, of what horrendous preserving fluids, they must have forced into his veins. Of course he would have looked fine as Fran had told us—the cosmeticians had covered the stroke-caused bruises and shaved a posthumous beard—but he was still dead, and I was still angry.

Sitting on a hillside one day overlooking a local canyon rich with the colors of autumn, I recounted to a friend the whole lurid story of my father's funeral and my indignation with the undertaker. We sipped homemade onion soup as I recited my newfound knowledge of all manner of disgusting practices such people perpetrate on unhappy relatives of the deceased. Did anyone care that "the staggering cost of dying" had outpaced the cost of living, that we as a nation were paying more to bury our dead than for all the costs incurred by our college students?

My good friend could only nod.

ॡ

---

[13] Words in quotes borrowed from Thomas Mallon's *New Yorker* review of Mitford's book.

I held onto this narrative of my father's death for a long time. Not until I started writing poetry some thirty years later did I revisit those scenes. In carefully counted syllables, I tried to dig beneath the anger to unearth my feelings about death and to mourn for my father. That first poem, "The Lonely Child" began with the airline strike and ended with a hope that I could "cull his melancholy days / into the handful of dirt" cast onto the humble man's coffin. That single page of well-disciplined lines acted as an exhumation, opening up a long-delayed and welcome examination of my feelings.

The anger, though justified, gave a convenient outlet for the disgust I felt toward myself. My attitudes of disdain and neglect had hurt my father. I think the inability to mourn came from a sense that I had no right to mourn.

I've rummaged boxes, both real and metaphoric, and filled many pages with draft after draft of angst. The fruit of these efforts ripened into what you have read here. I've looked my guilt and indifference in the eye and seen forgiveness.

⁓

I go up the flight of stairs and through the swinging doors into the print shop to face the father in whose widely-spaced eyes I can do no wrong. His workspace is still a special place for me. I sketch a floor plan, outlining every piece of equipment, every stone, every cluttered surface, just for the pleasure of remembering it. Remembering him. That quiet printer in his owlish glasses and ink-stained chambray shirt is my father. I like being his daughter.

This project has given me more time to be his daughter, to appreciate who and what he was before I was born. The memorabilia, newspapers, and letters helped me build a greater understanding and appreciation of his struggles, his aspirations and his joys. This chance to relive and tell the story of his life brought him closer to me. A rich lesson in printing.

EPILOGUE

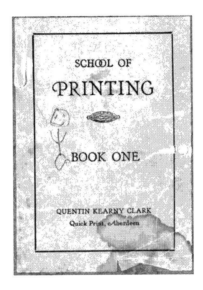

SCHOOL OF

PRINTING

BOOK ONE

QUENTIN KEARNY CLARK
Quick Print, Aberdeen

Wrapped for Delivery

It is not by any secret and mysterious methods, nor by supernatural gifts that successful printers produce work that is the wonder and envy of others; instead, it is the careful attention paid to these seemingly unimportant little things.
— Lessons in Printing

In the 1945 letter accompanying his brief will, my father wrote: "I hope, when it comes time for you to read this that you are all in good spirits and that you get all the best of the breaks that make up this thing called life." In his own way he supplied many of those breaks. He encouraged a love of family, of learning, of reading, and music. He chose as his wife a woman with the strength to endure and thrive no matter what threatened the family. I have to admire how well he covered a precarious mental state during my growing up and I'm grateful that I never had to undertake my avatar Ingeborg's dutiful return to her *Shelter Harbor* hometown to "save the business."

This modest man who likened himself to Popeye's 'I yam what I yam...,' wrote further, "Advice, I have none to give. That is the easiest stuff to dish out...the hardest to follow. But my dad used to tell us to try and do the right thing...to do the best you can." I have explored the stories buried in the rich collections of stuff those editors, my father and grandfather, left behind. I trust I was meant to follow in their footsteps, to honor their passage in "this thing called life."

❦

My archive is now just a collection of old paper. There are few things there, or in my house that I need to hand off to my children. The ghosts that haunt my ephemera are mine, not to be passed down the generations. Think about what the boxes can't contain: the taste of sea fog, smoke from a bonfire of alder leaves, the smell of scorched paper and kerosene rags in the print shop. Smoke rings from my father's pipe. That melancholy smile.

I can now celebrate the father revealed in these pages.

My hometown gave me what I needed. My father published a newspaper. We knew everyone. I was a big fish in a small pond. While Aberdeen never became a big port, it was a safe harbor for me. What more could one need than a well-watered town full of friends and relatives in a climate perfect for rhododendrons and azaleas, red cedar and Douglas fir.
Home.

cAcknowledgments

The author wishes to recognize her many teachers, mentors, and writing friends for their insightful and patient readings of many drafts: Sharon DeBartolo Carmack, Joan Coles, Beverley Cooper, Kathleen Farley, Franklin Fisher, Donna Graves, Karen Hayes, Robin Hemley, Andy Hoffman, David Kranes, Debbie Leaman, Lisa Linsalata, A.J. Martine, Michael Martone, Dawn Marano, Jerilyn McIntyre, Paisley Rekdal, Abigail Thomas, David Tippetts, Jennifer Tonge, and especially her husband, Noel de Nevers.

About the Type

The text of this book was set in Californian typeface. In 1938 Frederic Goudy designed the typeface California Oldstyle & Italic for the private use of the University of California Press; it was reissued in 1958 by Lanston Monotype Co. as Californian. Goudy was an enthusiast of the Arts & Crafts Movement and the works of William Morris. Many of his fonts were inspired by the old-style serif designs created between the fifteenth and eighteenth centuries. The digital version was released by ITC under its pre-existing brand as "Californian" by LTC and Font Bureau.

The titling font for this book is Heirloom Artcraft Demi Bold, designed in 2013 by Nathan Williams and published by Baseline Fonts. Its design approximates Artcraft URW Regular, a font used in many printshop and newspaper offices beginning in the 1920s. The cover labels that Kearny Clark printed for his copies of the *Lessons in Printing* series utilized that flourished Roman font. Heirloom Artcraft's similarly "swashed" capitals grace the title page and chapter titles in this, his daughter's book.

About the Author

Klancy de Nevers was born in Aberdeen, Washington, where her father's print shop inspired an abiding interest in words, newspapers and typography. She lives and writes in Salt Lake City. She is the author of *The Colonel and the Pacifist: Karl Bendetsen, Perry Saito and the Incarceration of Japanese Americans During World War II* and co-editor of *Cohassett Beach Chronicles: World War II in the Pacific Northwest* by Kathy Hogan, as well as a number of essays and poems. She may be reached through her website: Klancydenevers.com